# 10

## MINUTE GUIDE TO

# NETSCAPE FOR X WINDOWS

by Tim Evans

A Division of Macmillan Computer Publishing
201 West 103rd St., Indianapolis, Indiana 46290 USA

*For Tom and Raymond.*

## ©1995 by Que® Corporation

International Standard Book Number: 0-7897-0571-0

Library of Congress Catalog Card Number: 95-71041

98 97 96 95     8 7 6 5 4 3 2 1

Interpretation of the printing code: the rightmost double-digit number is the year of the book's first printing; the rightmost single-digit number is the number of the book's printing. For example, a printing code of 95-1 shows that this copy of the book was printed during the first printing of the book in 1995.

Screen reproductions in this book were created by means of John Cristy's program *ImageMagick*.

*Printed in the United States of America.*

**Publisher**  Roland Elgey

**Associate Publisher**  Stacy Hiquet

**Editorial Services Director**  Liz Keaffaber

**Managing Editor**  Sandy Doell

**Acquisitions Editor**  Beverly Eppink

**Development Editor**  Benjamin Milstead

**Editor**  Kelly Oliver

**Technical Editor**  Tobin Anthony

**Technical Specialist**  Cari Skaggs

**Book Designer**  Barbara Kordesh

**Cover Design**  Scott Cook

**Indexer**  Debra Myers

**Production**  Angela Bannan, Becky Beheler, Lisa Daugherty, Joan Evan, Amy Gornik, Jason Hand, John Hulse, Clint Lahnen, Laura Robbins, Bobbi Satterfield, Craig Small, Michael Thomas, Kelly Warner, and Todd Wente

# ABOUT THE AUTHOR

**Tim Evans**, also the author of Que's *10 Minute Guide to HTML*, is a UNIX system administration and network security consultant. Employed by Taratec Development Corporation, his full-time contract assignment for the past three years has been at the DuPont Company's Experimental Station in Wilmington, Delaware. He pioneered development of DuPont's own world-wide web, known as DuPont-Wide Web, widely used within the company for information sharing via its world-wide network. Previously, Tim worked for the U.S. Social Security Administration in various staff jobs for more than 20 years. In 1991, before the Internet got hot, he brought that government agency onto the Internet. At both DuPont and SSA, he provided support for large numbers of UNIX users, running UNIX on a variety of computer systems, ranging from PCs to workstations to mini-computers.

A native of Missouri, Tim is a former carny (he had his own merry-go-round to operate at age 14), auto assembly line worker, janitor, and bartender. His degrees in History show a Liberal Arts education can qualify you for almost any job, depending on what you do afterward. Tim also is a produced playwright with an extensive background in community theatre, both on and off stage. He lives with his wife and best friend, Carol, and their Irish Setter, Judy! Judy! Judy!, in Delaware, just three hours from their vacation home in Chincoteague, VA. He can be reached via Internet e-mail at *tkevans@dupont.com*.

# ACKNOWLEDGMENTS

The screenshots in this book were captured and manipulated with John Cristy's set of UNIX imaging utilities, *ImageMagick*. Special thanks to C$^2$E and Karen Bloch for file conversions under particularly difficult circumstances. Thanks also to Beverly Eppink, Tobin Anthony, Andrea Duvall, Ben Milstead, and Kelly Oliver of Que Publishing for their support—and for going the important extra miles.

# CONTENTS

# Introduction

Netscape Navigator seems to be taking the World Wide Web by storm. Statistics seem to show Netscape dominating the Web browser market, with anywhere from 60 to 75 percent share. Netscape Communications Corporation's initial public stock offering made front-page news, with the stock soaring more than 200 percent in their first couple of hours of trading. It's pretty amazing that any software package can gain anything like this sort of market share in just a year's time, but Netscape's done just that.

## What Is Netscape?

Netscape is computer software for browsing the World Wide Web. Since you're using a UNIX computer system, you may already be using a Web browser, such as NCSA Mosaic, so you're pretty familiar with the Web. Netscape provides the features of other Web browsers—along with features of its own—in an attractive and easy-to-use package. If you compare Mosaic to your basic Chevy, you might see Netscape as a bright red Corvette: both provide transportation, but the Corvette may be more fun to drive.

Moreover, like some TV shows (*Northern Exposure* or possibly anything on *MTV* come to mind), Netscape has a definite attitude. Many people find Netscape irresistible. Others, of course, are perfectly happy watching *Murder, She Wrote*. You probably already know which sort of person you are, and you'll learn what we mean as you learn about Netscape. You'll want to keep an open mind, though, especially if you're a businessperson or other professional who's looking for a professional tool. Netscape's seemingly adolescent outlook on things can be off-putting. Don't let this get in the way of your realization that the package may be just the tool you need. After all, success is as success does, and no one can argue with Netscape's success.

# What Is the 10 Minute Guide and Why Do You Need It?

This book is one of Que's three *10 Minute Guides* to Netscape. (The others are dedicated to Netscape on Macintosh and IBM-compatible/Windows PCs, respectively.) Netscape is similar on the three computer platforms, but each is different enough that you'll want the *10 Minute Guide* for the system(s) you use.

Netscape runs on a wide variety of UNIX systems, including Sun Microsystems, IBM, Digital, Silicon Graphics, Hewlett-Packard, and others. This *10 Minute Guide* focuses on the version of Netscape for UNIX systems running the X Window system.

The *10 Minute Guide to Netscape for X Windows* uses a series of lessons to walk you through the basics of Netscape and then moves on to more advanced features. Each lesson is designed to take you about 10 minutes to work through, and each is limited to a particular feature, or several related features, of the package. If you've used a Web browser before, you'll find many things about Netscape familiar, since you already have a basic understanding of the World Wide Web.

If you haven't used a Web browser, you'll still find these lessons accessible, and you'll get a good introduction to the Web. There are plenty of examples and figures that show you what things look like. By the time you finish this book, you'll be an advanced Netscape user.

# Do I Have to Know A Lot About UNIX?

No. If you're like many people who use UNIX systems, you're familiar with the basics, like how to use your windowing system—moving windows around, clicking icons to start programs, and so on. You probably also know a bit about entering simple shell commands and using a simple text editor. This basic knowledge, along with a general familiarity with the system of directories and subdirectories used on UNIX systems, is all I'll assume in this book. Your system administrator can help with the installation and setup of Netscape; he may already have done so for you.

 **System Administrator?** Unlike PC operating systems, UNIX systems are multi-user, multi-tasking computers. Since they're more complex than PCs, UNIX systems usually need trained system administrators to maintain them.

# X WINDOWS

Netscape for UNIX runs under the X Windows system, often called just X. All the UNIX vendors on whose systems Netscape runs provide X, but they often give it a fancy name. Sun calls it OpenWindows; IBM, AIXWindows; and Hewlett-Packard, VUE. Rest assured, if Netscape is running on your system, it's running under X. What's important about X Windows in the context of Netscape is Netscape *looks and acts the same on all the different UNIX systems it supports*. Setup and configuration are the same and the appearance of the screens are the same. All the figures in this book were captured on an IBM RISC/6000 system running AIX, but they'd look exactly alike on a Sun, SGI, or HP. As a result, everything you already know about using the windowing system on your UNIX machine is directly usable in Netscape.

# ICONS AND CONVENTIONS USED IN THIS BOOK

The following icons have been added throughout the book to help you find your way around:

 Timesaver Tip icons offer shortcuts and hints for using the program efficiently.

Plain English icons define new terms.

Panic Button icons appear where new users often run into trouble.

Words or phrases printed in blue serve a double purpose: first, they're printed in blue the first time they're used, and second, they represent a command you type, an icon, or a click-button.

The following conventions have been used to clarify the steps you must perform:

| | |
|---|---|
| **On-screen text** | Any text that appears on-screen appears in bold type. |
| **What you type** | The information you type appears in bold color type. |
| Press Enter | Keys you press (or selections you make with the mouse) appear in color type. |
| Key+Key Combinations | In many cases, you must press a two-key key combination in order to enter a command. For example, "Press Alt+X." In such cases, hold down the first key while pressing the second key. |

## TRADEMARKS

All terms mentioned in this book that are known to be trademarks or service marks are appropriately capitalized. The Que Corporation cannot attest to the accuracy of this information. Use of a term in this book should not be regarded as affecting the validity of any trademark or service mark.

# STARTING AND EXITING NETSCAPE

*In this lesson, you'll learn how to start and exit Netscape. You will also learn about the Netscape screen and home page, and how to get help online.*

## STARTING NETSCAPE

Before you start Netscape, you should understand what it is. Netscape for UNIX is a program for browsing the World Wide Web, and runs under X Windows. X Windows (or just "X") is the generic name for the graphical user interface (GUI) provided by most UNIX system vendors. X goes by different names—IBM calls it AIXWindows; Sun, OpenWindows; and Hewlett-Packard, VUE, to give several examples. (In the near future, these and other vendors' versions of X will merge as the Common Desktop Environment.) We'll use the generic *X Windows* or just *X* to refer to the X GUI you're running.

You must have the X Windows GUI running to run Netscape. Typical UNIX commands to start up X, if it's not already running, are xinit, startx, or (on Sun systems) openwin. Check with your system administrator for help getting X started. As is the case with so many other UNIX programs, there are several ways of starting Netscape. The simplest is to start it from your shell prompt in a terminal window, such as anxterm, cmdtool, aixterm, hpterm, and so on, like this:

**$ netscape &**

**Shell? Terminal Window?** While many UNIX programs are available by clicking an icon (as in other GUIs), many users also open terminal windows, providing access to the UNIX command interpreter, the shell. In the preceding example, the dollar sign is the UNIX shell prompt. Your X Windows environment provides a pull-down menu from which you can select a terminal window.

The ampersand symbol (**&**) used in the command tells UNIX to start Netscape but also return your shell prompt by placing the program in the background. UNIX is a multi-tasking operating system; you can run many jobs at the same time.

When you enter the **netscape &** command, the program starts and displays Netscape's home page (see Figure 1.1). If this is the first time you start Netscape, you will see the license agreement before the home page.

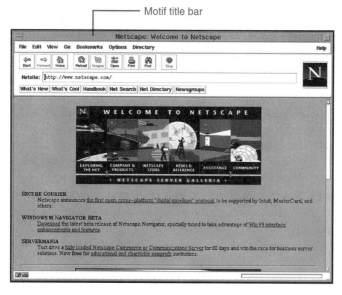

Motif title bar

**FIGURE 1.1**   Netscape's home page.

**Home Page**   Your home page is the first screen you see when Netscape starts up. Usually, this is a page on the World Wide Web. Netscape comes preconfigured to start up with Netscape Communications Corporation's startup page, but you can set it up to start anywhere at all—or nowhere.

**Where's Netscape's Home Page?**   If you start Netscape and the Netscape page isn't displayed, there are several possible explanations. Your system administrator may have preconfigured Netscape to point to some other home page, such as a local one. It may have been set to point to no home page at all (in which case, you'll see an informational page about Netscape). You may have local area network problems, or there could be trouble on the Internet.

## NETSCAPE AND MOTIF—A QUICK LESSON FOR SUN USERS

Netscape is a Motif X Windows program. *Motif* is one of two flavors of X, and it governs how windows look and how you interact with them using your mouse. Most UNIX vendors' versions of X Windows use the Motif interface.

Sun's OpenWindows GUI is not a Motif interface. If you're a Sun user, you'll find some new things about Motif's title bar (shown in Figure 1.1). You're accustomed to the OpenLook Window menu (which is a non-Motif interface), accessible from the triangle on the upper left. This menu has changed in Motif, as has the symbol in the title bar for getting it—it's now a horizontal bar, still on the upper left. Clicking it opens the Motif Window menu, with options for moving, resizing, and closing the window. Minimize has replaced OpenLook's Close, and Maximize has replaced Full Size. Minimize reduces the window to an icon, while Maximize causes the window to occupy the full screen.

**Motif Shortcuts**   The Motif title bar also has a couple of shortcuts. Note the upper right, where you'll see a dot and a raised box. Clicking on the dot minimizes the window, and clicking the raised box maximizes it. Once maximized, the raised box is shown depressed; clicking it again restores the window to its original size.

If you think Motif looks like Microsoft Windows on a PC, you're right. The X Windows GUI war is over: Sun Microsystems' CEO Scott McNealy finally said the M word—you'll see Motif on future releases of Solaris, Sun's version of UNIX. Eventually, Open-Windows will be obsolete.

## Understanding Netscape Screen Parts

Figure 1.2 shows the important parts of Netscape's window that are listed below. These will be covered in detail in this and future lessons.

- **Location**   Displays the location of the Web page you are viewing.

- **Status Indicator**   The "N" icon displays streaming meteors to indicate some level of activity (such as copying a picture that is part of the current screen, copying additional text that isn't appearing on your screen yet, and so on), usually while a Web page is being read by your computer.

- **Progress Bar**   Displays a red bar to indicate the progress of reading a page or copying a file to your computer (called *downloading*).

- **Toolbar**   Displays Netscape's most commonly used commands.

- **Directory Buttons**   These are preset to jump you to other useful pages on the Web.

- **Security Indicator**   Indicates whether the current page meets security criteria. (See Lesson 19 for details on Netscape security.)

- **Status Message**   Shows messages of importance to you from Netscape.

- **Link**   Another page you can jump to; it is usually indicated by a different color and/or underlined text.

- **Security Colorbars**   Another type of security indicator.

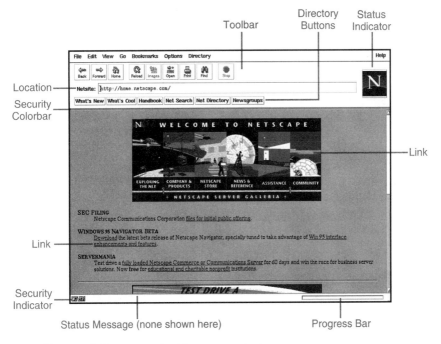

**FIGURE 1.2**   Parts of a Netscape window.

# GETTING HELP ONLINE

Although you can purchase a printed manual, help for Netscape—including the full text of the printed manual—is available online. Help is available through the Help menu (see Figure 1.3).

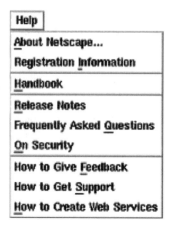

**FIGURE 1.3** Netscape's Help menu.

Netscape provides a lot of information on its Help menu. There are listings on Registration, Release Notes, and Security. Detailed help is found under Handbook (see Figure 1.4) and Frequently Asked Questions, also known as FAQs (see Figure 1.5). These two documents are actually Web pages at Netscape Communications Corp.; they're always up-to-date.

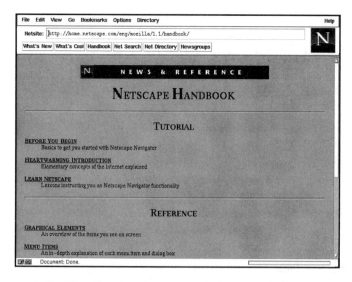

**FIGURE 1.4** The Handbook section of Netscape Help.

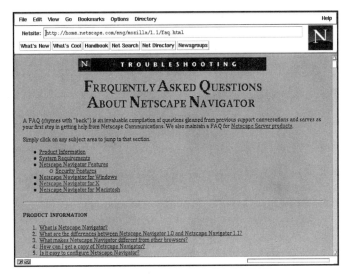

**FIGURE 1.5** The Frequently Asked Questions section of Netscape Help.

 **FAQ** Frequently Asked Questions are common questions that come up over and over again. Netscape has attempted to put together a list of them, along with answers, with this link.

## QUITTING NETSCAPE

To quit Netscape, open the File menu and click Exit. Alternatively, you can press Alt+W. Because you're running on a UNIX system, you may want to leave Netscape running but reduce it to an icon for later reopening. To do so, just click the dot in the upper right of the Netscape title bar (just like minimizing any other Motif window). Later, you can reopen Netscape by double-clicking the Netscape icon.

In this lesson, you learned how to start and quit Netscape and about the parts of its screen. In the next lesson, you will learn how to use Netscape's Toolbar to navigate through the Web.

# 2 NAVIGATING AND JUMPING TO YOUR FIRST WEB SITE

*In this lesson, you learn about Netscape's Toolbar and how to use the four navigational icons.*

## WHAT IS THE TOOLBAR?

Netscape's Toolbar is a set of icons that quickly execute the most commonly used commands in Netscape. For example, any time you want to return to your home page, you click the icon labeled Home.

The Toolbar is located near the top of the Netscape screen. The nine Netscape Toolbar icons appear in the following table, along with a brief explanation of what each one does.

| ICON | ACTION |
|------|--------|
| Back | Moves back to previously visited page. |
| Forward | Moves forward to previously visited page. |
| Home | Displays your home page. |
| Reload | Reloads previously visited page. |
| Images | Displays images onto current page if they were not loaded automatically. |
| Open | Opens the Open Location dialog box, in which you enter a new URL. |

*continues*

*continued*

| ICON | ACTION |
|------|--------|
|  Print | Prints the currently displayed page. |
| Find | Finds text in the current page. |
| Stop | Stops ongoing transfer of Web page. |

# USING THE NAVIGATIONAL ICONS

Of these nine icons, Back, Forward, Home, and Reload are navigational icons. They help you move around on the Web.

Let's take a closer look now at how the navigational icons work. For reasons you'll come to understand, we won't proceed in the order in which the four icons are shown on the Toolbar. The rest of the Toolbar icons will be covered in the next lesson.

## USING THE OPEN ICON TO JUMP TO WEB SITES

The Open icon jumps you to a new page on the World Wide Web (from now on, it will be referred to simply as the Web). Here's how it works:

1. Click the Open icon. The Open Location dialog box appears (see Figure 2.1).

FIGURE 2.1    The Open Location dialog box.

**2.** Type the following URL to go to the U.S. White House home page:

**http://www.whitehouse.gov/**

 **URL** URL stands for Uniform Resource Locator, which is a standard way of describing the *location* of a page or other resource on the Web or on the Internet. In this context, it doesn't matter if the page is on your own computer or one in the next state or two continents away. URLs also describe the *type of data* the resource or page represents. Netscape and other Web browsers, such as Mosaic, use URLs to locate and interpret Web pages and other Internet resources.

**3.** Click Open, or just press Enter. In a few seconds, the White House home page appears on your screen (see Figure 2.2).

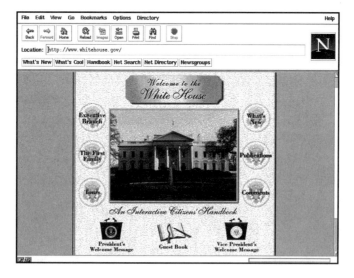

**FIGURE 2.2**    The White House home page.

**The White House Did Not Appear!**   URLs are *case-sensitive*, so make sure you typed it exactly as shown. Also note that forward slashes (//) are used, not backslashes (\\).

If you're still having trouble after verifying the URL, there are any number of possible explanations for a temporary inability to reach a given URL. The remote computer may be down for maintenance or because of a power failure. There may be network problems at your site or on the Internet somewhere between your site and the White House. Very busy Web servers, like the White House's, may be too busy to respond to your connection at a given time. If your network administrator tells you there are no local network problems, try again in a few minutes.

Click the Guest Book icon, just below the legend *An Interactive Citizens' Handbook*. (You may need to use the vertical scroll bar, located on the right side of the screen, to scroll down to just below the picture of the White House.) This takes you to the Guest Book page (see Figure 2.3).

As you can see, this is a fill-in form, in which you can type your name and a message for the White House. Hold off for the moment on filling in your message while you learn more about Netscape navigation. You'll come back to this page later.

## NAVIGATING WITH THE BACK AND FORWARD ICONS

Back and Forward are most useful after you have viewed a series of pages. The Back icon takes you back to the last page you visited. If you're following along, you're still viewing the White House Guest Book page. Click Back to backtrack to the White House home page.

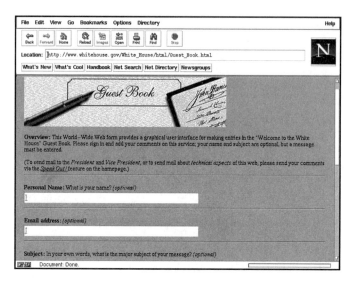

**FIGURE 2.3**   The White House Guest Book page.

Now click Forward to go to the Guest Book page. As you can see, the Forward icon takes you forward one page through a list of already visited pages. At this point, your list of visited pages is only three pages long—your home page, the White House home page and the Guest Book page—but you probably get the idea. Later (in Lesson 5), you'll learn how to use Back and Forward in conjunction with Netscape's History command to step through a longer list of pages.

If you'd like, return to the Guest Book page by clicking Back once again and "sign" the guest book, where you can also leave a message for U.S. President Bill Clinton or his family.

## RETURNING HOME

The Home icon returns you to your home page. Netscape comes preconfigured to access the Netscape Communications Corp.'s home page, which is what you see when you first start the program. (Turn back to Lesson 1 and look at Figure 1.1 for a picture of the Netscape home page.) You'll learn in Lesson 24 how to set the Home icon to return to your own home page, or how to set no home page at all.

For now, click Home to return to Netscape's home page.

**Back or Home?**  If you're thinking you could've used Back to get back to your home page, you're right. However, you'd have had to click Back *twice* to get from the White House Guest Book page to your home page. The Home icon always takes you directly to your home page.

## EXPLORING ON YOUR OWN

Now that you know about Netscape's four navigational icons, you may want to do some exploring on your own before going to the next lesson. Click Open and try visiting a few of the Web sites listed on the inside front and back covers. Each listing has the site's URL; just type it in. This will also give you some practice using the Forward and Back icons.

In this lesson, you learned how to use the four navigational icons in Netscape. In the next lesson, you'll learn how to use the remaining Toolbar icons.

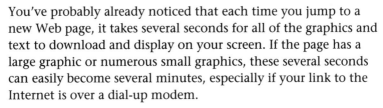

# USING NON-NAVIGATIONAL ICONS ON THE TOOLBAR

*In this lesson, you'll learn about the Netscape Toolbar's other icons—the "non-navigational" icons.*

In Lesson 2, you learned about the icons on Netscape's Toolbar, especially the icons for navigating the Web. In this lesson, you'll learn about the "non-navigational" icons: Stop, Reload, Images, Print, and Find. Again, we're taking them in a logical order, rather than following them across the Toolbar.

## USING THE STOP ICON

You've probably already noticed that each time you jump to a new Web page, it takes several seconds for all of the graphics and text to download and display on your screen. If the page has a large graphic or numerous small graphics, these several seconds can easily become several minutes, especially if your link to the Internet is over a dial-up modem.

If the transfer takes a very long time, you might not want to wait for all of the graphics, especially if you are revisiting a Web page. The Stop icon—shaped like a highway stop sign—allows you to interrupt the transfer, or *download*, of a Web page. The Stop icon is normally dimmed out in Netscape, but while you're download-ing a Web page it turns red to indicate you can use it. Since Netscape downloads the text of Web pages first, you can display the text after clicking the Stop icon.

**Download**   To copy a file from another computer to yours. When you jump to a new Web page in Netscape, it downloads the text and graphic files in that page to your computer so they can be displayed.

When a file is downloading, you'll see its progress in the Status Message line, which is at the bottom of your screen. It will look like this:

**Document Received xxxx of yyyy bytes.**

The first number (*xxxx*) will increase in increments as more of the file is received. The second number (*yyyy*) shows the size of the file you're downloading. Together, the numbers give you an idea of how long it will take to complete the download.

## USING THE RELOAD ICON

You'll learn in Lesson 6 that Netscape saves the pages you download on your local system disk for a short time. If you need to access them again soon, access time is quicker because the pages don't have to be downloaded again. Sometimes pages change, though, and you may want to ensure you have the latest version. Reload does this for you. You can also use Reload when you've interrupted a download with the Stop icon. Here's an example that shows how to use both Stop and Reload:

1. Click Open (to open a location on the Web). In the Open dialog box, type this URL:

   **http://www.umkc.edu/**

2. While the counter is increasing in increments, quickly click the Stop icon to interrupt the transfer. Your screen should look something like Figure 3.1. As you can see, there's text you can read, but the images may not have downloaded or may have partially downloaded.

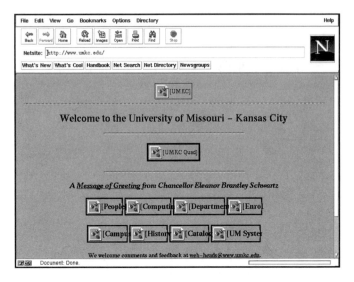

**FIGURE 3.1**   An interrupted transfer of a Web Page after clicking the Stop icon.

**3.** Now click Reload to reload the stopped page. When the full page is completely downloaded, you'll see the home page shown in Figure 3.2, which is the home page of the University of Missouri—Kansas City.

# IMAGE LOADING

You'll learn in Lesson 24 you can suppress the automatic loading/display of images on Web pages. (This is particularly useful if your connection to the Internet is via a dial-up modem or other slow link.) If you've set up Netscape to suppress image loading, clicking the Images icon on the toolbar allows you to bring up the images on the current page when you want to see them.

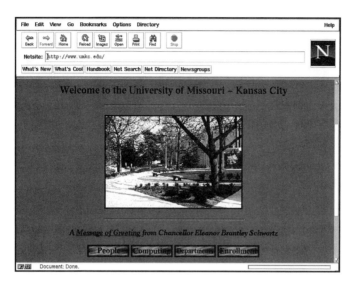

FIGURE 3.2    The UMKC home page.

# LOCATING TEXT STRINGS WITH FIND

Many computer programs, such as word processors, have a valuable feature that allows you to search for text strings, including words and phrases, in a document. Netscape's Find does this in the Web page you're viewing. Here's how it works:

1. Click Open and type this URL:

   **http:/www.mit.edu/**

   This takes you to the home page of the Massachusetts Institute of Technology.

2. Click Find to display the Find dialog box, as shown in Figure 3.3.

3. Type the letters **mit** and press Enter, or click Find. Netscape finds the first instance of the letters *mit*, highlighting the located text.

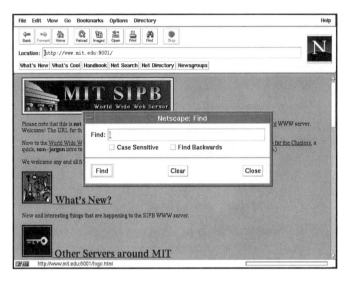

**FIGURE 3.3**    The Find dialog box.

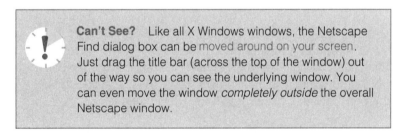

**Can't See?**    Like all X Windows windows, the Netscape Find dialog box can be moved around on your screen. Just drag the title bar (across the top of the window) out of the way so you can see the underlying window. You can even move the window *completely outside* the overall Netscape window.

**4.** Continue clicking Find to look for additional instances of the search string.

If you see **Search String Not Found!**, it means all instances of the designated text have been found. You'll also notice that in the Find dialog box you can search backward as well as forward. You can also select the Case Sensitive check box if you are looking for an exact match. When you're finished with the Find dialog box, click Close to exit.

# PRINTING WEB PAGES

The Print icon does just what you would expect: it prints the current page, just as you see it on-screen. UNIX systems usually have the capability of accessing several printers on your local network, so you need a way of telling Netscape where to print your job, as well as some other information. UNIX Netscape therefore has a Print dialog box, shown in Figure 3.4.

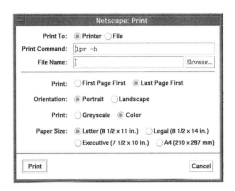

**FIGURE 3.4**    Netscape's Print dialog box.

As you can see, there are quite a few choices here. Let's start at the top and run through them quickly. First, you have the choice of sending your printout to a Printer or to a print File, with the printer pre-selected. (If printing to a file, fill in the File Name box.)

Since you probably want to print your page now, take a look at the Print Command box. (The contents of this box on your system may differ slightly from Figure 3.4.) If you have only one printer on your system or want to print to your usual printer, just leave the command as is. Some PostScript printers print documents from front to back, but the pages land in the output tray with the last page on top. If your printer is like this, select Last Page First.

There's no reason to tell Netscape to print in color if your printer is not a color printer; select Greyscale or Color, as appropriate. You can also check off your printer's Paper Size.

Finally, click Print to ship the page off to the printer, using the print criteria selected.

**Print Error**   If Netscape gives you an error message when you try to print, double-check the print command you entered or check with your system administrator.

In this lesson, you learned how to use the remaining Toolbar icons. In the next lesson, you will learn about hyperlinks and how to move through a Web page.

# USING HYPERLINKS TO MOVE THROUGH A WEB PAGE

*In this lesson, you will learn about World Wide Web hyperlinks and how to move through Web pages.*

## UNDERSTANDING HYPERLINKS AND HYPERTEXT

You've probably realized Web pages are not merely isolated documents. The vast majority of pages contain connections to other Web pages. These connections are called hyperlinks. Following hyperlinks that look interesting leads you to more Web pages—possibly with further hyperlinks. If you think about it, this is a new way of accessing information. Encyclopedias and other reference documents are arranged in a hierarchical fashion. Cross-references exist, but you have to use the hierarchical arrangement of the reference work to locate the cross-references.

The World Wide Web uses a different way of managing information called hypertext. Hypertext, along with the hyperlinks it includes, lets you get to information in a more intuitive way than a rigid hierarchical organization. Following hyperlinks lets you select what appears interesting to you in a document and get more information about it. As you'll see, hyperlinks in Web documents allow you to point and click your way around the Web in your own way, following links as they seem interesting. This is the way many people think, so using hypertext comes pretty naturally, though some literal-minded folks grouse about the way hypertext—and the Web—is horribly disorganized.

## Identifying Hyperlinks

When using Netscape, most hyperlinks are easy to identify. Let's go to a Web page with lots of hyperlinks. Click Open and go to:

**http://cirrus.sprl.umich.edu/wxnet/**

This is *WeatherNet* (see Figure 4.1).

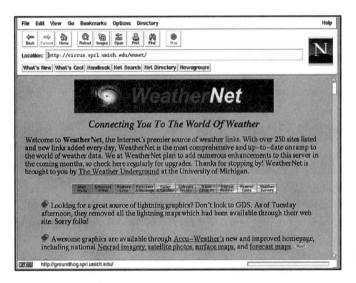

**Figure 4.1**    WeatherNet.

Notice that some of the words and phrases in this page are underlined; if you have a color monitor, they also appear in a different color than the rest of the text. These are hyperlinks. (In Lesson 24, you'll learn how to change the way hyperlinks appear on-screen using Netscape Preferences.) If you move your mouse cursor to the underlined text, Netscape displays the URL of the link on the status message line. (See the lower left corner of Figure 4.1.)

# WHAT IS A UNIFORM RESOURCE LOCATOR?

The *Uniform Resource Locator*, or URL, is the key to locating and interpreting information on the Internet. As you learned in Lesson 2, URLs are a standard way of describing both the location of a Web resource and its content. URLs help you locate Web resources, regardless of whether a resource is another document on your local computer or a file on another computer halfway around the world.

Let's use a fictional company's home page as an example to demonstrate the three parts to an URL:

**http://www.mycompany.com/home.html.**

- Service Name is followed by a colon and *two* forward slashes. In the example URL, the service name is http.

- Internet hostname is where the service is located and optional port number, followed by a single forward slash. In the example URL, www.mycompany.com is the Internet hostname.

- Resource is normally a document or file on the computer, but there are also other kinds of resources. In the example URL, home.html is the resource—in this case, a home page.

 **Port Numbers**   Internet services use imaginary wires to connect services between imaginary plugs (*ports*) on two computers. These virtual connections are managed by the network software using an abstraction called *port numbers.*

# MOVING AROUND ON A WEB PAGE

Many Web pages take no more than a single Netscape screen to display, but others are longer. Netscape has a scroll bar, which lets you move through a longer page. Just move your mouse cursor to the scroll bar, *left-click* on the bar, and then pull it down (or up) to move around the page. You can also click the up and down scroll bar anchors (the little triangles at the top and bottom) to move more slowly. All the Netscape screenshots in this book show the scroll bar on the right side of the window, but this is something left-handed users can change. You may also find some Web pages that are too wide to display all at once. In these cases, a horizontal scroll bar will appear at the bottom of the window; use it to move the screen left or right.

# ACCESSING HYPERLINKS

To follow a hyperlink, just move your mouse cursor to it and click. Let's try a couple of hyperlinks on the WeatherNet home page. Scroll down to World Wide Web Servers, and then click EarthWatch Communications (see Figure 4.2).

Next, scroll down to Satellite Imagery. Here, you'll see a new kind of hyperlink. Look carefully and you'll see that not only is the text *Satellite Imagery* highlighted on your screen, but the image immediately to its left is also outlined in the same highlight color. This means you can follow this hyperlink by clicking either on the highlighted text, as you've learned, or *right on the image* of the satellite view of North America (see Figure 4.3).

Let's follow one more hyperlink, and then regroup. Select the hyperlink for the Eastern United States. (Click the word HERE.) Figure 4.4 shows this page. The Location, Directory Buttons, and Toolbar have been temporarily removed to show you more of the image. What you see will be a little different from Figure 4.4; you'll learn about suppressing the Toolbar, Directory Buttons, and/or Location in Lesson 23.

**FIGURE 4.2**   EarthWatch Communications' home page.

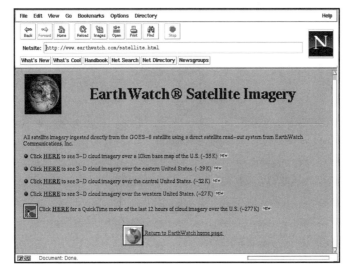

**FIGURE 4.3**   EarthWatch® Satellite Imagery.

**FIGURE 4.4**    Cloud imagery over the eastern United States.

    **Some Links Don't Work**   The World Wide Web changes rapidly. Some of the example links in this book may no longer work by the time you read it. Just click Back to return to the previous page.

# TRACING YOUR HYPERLINKS

You've now been through a trail of Web pages. Now's a good time to review using the Back and Forward icons you learned about in Lesson 2.

To see where you've been in this Netscape session, click Back three times. On each previous page, you'll notice that the link you visited earlier has changed color. This is how Netscape shows hyperlinks you've visited. Normally, Netscape will maintain these link-visit indicators for 30 days, but you'll learn in Lesson 24 how to change this to suit your own way of using Netscape.

Now, click a few times on the Forward icon, and you'll step forward through the pages you've visited. Did you notice these pages displayed a lot quicker than before? That's because Netscape *caches*, or stores, each page you visit during each online session. If you revisit a cached page, Netscape grabs the page from the local disk instead of over the Web. Unfortunately, this feature does not carry over from one session to another. You'll learn more about Netscape's cache feature in Lesson 6.

In this lesson, you learned how to move through a Web page and what hyperlinks are. In the next lesson you will learn how to use Netscape's History feature.

# USING HISTORY TO SEE WHERE YOU'VE BEEN

*In this lesson, you will learn to use Netscape's History feature.*

In Lesson 4, you learned how to find hyperlinks on a Web page and that these hyperlinks are often connections to other Web pages. Also, you learned that by clicking a hyperlink you can jump to that Web page. You've also used Back and Forward to move through a trail of the Web pages you've visited.

## USING NETSCAPE'S HISTORY FEATURE

Using Back and Forward is fine if you just want to revisit a page you've just visited, but what if you want to go back *several* pages? Repeatedly clicking Back or Forward can become tedious—there's another way. Netscape keeps a trail of the Web pages you've visited. This trail is called History. This feature allows you not only to track where you've been, but also to jump back to any Web page you've visited in a Netscape session with just a couple of mouse clicks.

To see how Netscape's History feature works, let's build such a trail of Web pages first. Begin with a Web site that provides many hyperlinks to other Web sites: the Smithsonian Institution in Washington, D.C. Click Open and go to this URL:

**http://www.si.edu/**

This will take you to the Smithsonian Home Page (see Figure 5.1).

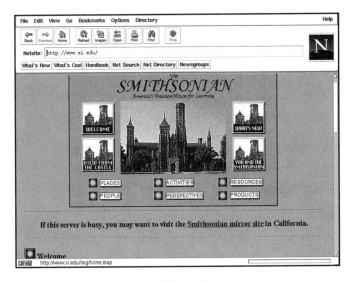

**FIGURE 5.1**   The Smithsonian Home Page.

This pages demonstrates an important Web feature called a clickable image map.

> **Image Map**   Look carefully at Figure 5.1, and you'll see the large image is highlighted; it is itself a hyperlink. Clickable image maps are special Web page images that allow you to click somewhere within the image and access a Web page; clicking somewhere else in the image gets you a different page.

Now that you know about clickable image maps, click the part of the image labeled What's New. Next, click New and Temporary Exhibitions. From the list of bullets on the next page, select National Air and Space Museum. You should now be at the page shown in Figure 5.2.

**FIGURE 5.2**   The New and Temporary Exhibition at the National Air and Space Museum.

Now click the link at the upper left that says National Air and Space Museum. When the next page appears, you'll be at the National Air and Space Museum Home Page (see Figure 5.3).

You've jumped from one Web page to the next, and we've almost reached our destination. At the very bottom of this page, click Resources. (It's second from the right in the blue button bar.) At the next page, scroll down to Smithsonian Photos and click that link. Figure 5.4 shows this final page.

You've been through a possibly tedious and convoluted journey, but you've been building a Netscape History. Let's see how it works. Pull down the Netscape Go menu, where you'll see a history of your trek in this lesson. (See Figure 5.5.)

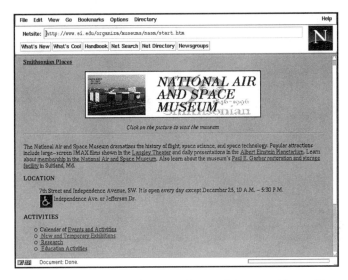

FIGURE 5.3    The National Air and Space Museum Home Page.

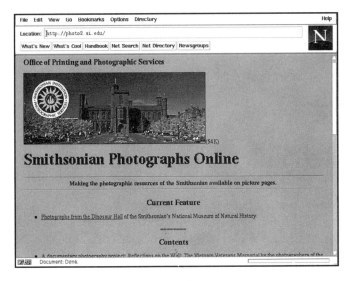

FIGURE 5.4    The Smithsonian Photographs Online page.

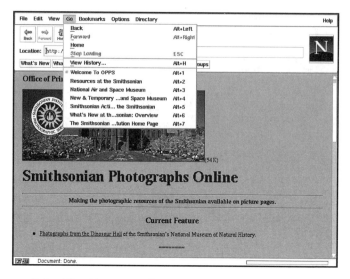

**FIGURE 5.5**    The Netscape Go menu with History shown.

Here you see a list of all the Web pages you've visited in this lesson (and possibly in the prior lessons if you've done this all in one session). Some of the pages' titles are abbreviated to fit into the box. You can pop back to any of them by dragging your mouse down through the list to highlight the one you want and releasing the mouse button. (Note also that Alt-key combinations will work.)

To get more detail on your Netscape History, with information like full URL listings, select View History; you'll get a pop-up like the one in Figure 5.6.

Single-click on one of the pages, and then select Go To to jump directly back to that page. (Alternatively, just double-click the page you want.) We'll save the Create Bookmark box until the next lesson, but you can probably guess what it means.

Netscape will keep accumulating items in your History until you exit the program, so your History list can get quite long. You may wonder how many History items Netscape can keep track of at one time. The answer depends on, among other things, how

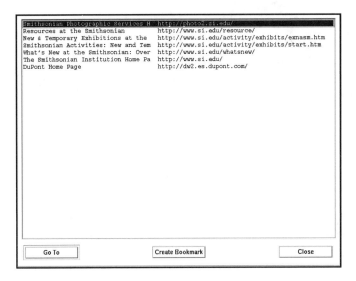

**FIGURE 5.6**    Netscape's History window.

much free disk space you have on your computer and how much of that disk space you are willing to let Netscape use. We'll cover how Netscape makes use of your free disk space in Lesson 22.

## TAKE A BREAK

By now, you probably feel like a typical Washington, D.C. tourist. You've taken a whirlwind tour of the Smithsonian Institution and need a break. Before you go to the next lesson, you might want to spend some time looking at some of the Web pages on your History list. You'll find some outstanding photographs and other great Web resources, just as you would exploring the Smithsonian on foot.

In this lesson, you learned how to use Netscape's History feature. In the next lesson you'll learn how to keep a permanent record of your travels by using Netscape's Bookmark feature.

# CREATING AND USING BOOKMARKS

*In this lesson, you will learn how to make a permanent record of interesting Web pages in Netscape so you can return to them easily.*

In the last lesson, you learned that Netscape maintains a History list of Web pages you visit and allows you to use this list to jump quickly backward and forward among them. Unfortunately, this list is only temporary, *lasting only as long as your Netscape session.* All the interesting sites you visited—and which were recorded in your History—disappear when you exit Netscape.

## UNDERSTANDING BOOKMARKS

However, Netscape does offer a way to permanently record Web pages you find interesting. This is the Netscape Bookmark. Like a traditional bookmark, Netscape's Bookmark feature places a special marker tracked by the software. Bookmarks allow you to turn back to a specific place. This marker records the URL of a Web page, its name, the date you added the page to your Bookmark list, and the last time you visited the site.

Later, when you want to revisit a particular Web page, you can ask Netscape for a list of your Bookmarks, from which you can select the page you want quickly and easily.

## CREATING BOOKMARKS

While Netscape will automatically place Web sites in its History list, if you want Web sites placed in your Bookmark list, you have to add them yourself. It's a simple, straightforward procedure.

Before starting, exit from Netscape, and then restart it to clear
your History list. Now, let's go to several new Web pages and
place a Bookmark for each.

Open **http://www.ibm.com**. This will take you to the home
page of International Business Machines—IBM (see Figure 6.1).

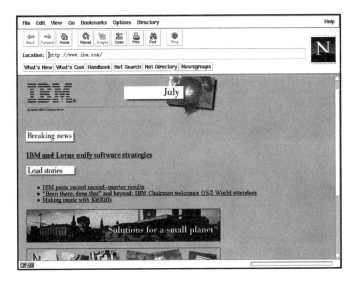

FIGURE 6.1    IBM's home page.

**The Page Looks Different from the Screenshot**   Many
companies update/redesign their Web pages on a regular
basis to keep them fresh. What you see on-screen is the
current page, rather than the one shown in Figure 6.1.

Select the Netscape Bookmarks menu, and then select Add Bookmark. See Figure 6.2, which is an enlarged portion of Figure 6.1,
showing the Bookmarks menu. This places the current Web
page—in this case, the IBM home page—on your Bookmark list.

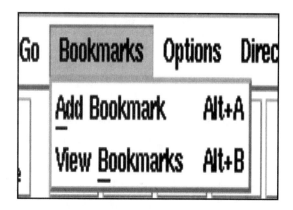

FIGURE 6.2    The Bookmark menu.

Let's add several more pages to your Bookmarks. Repeat this process with the following Web pages, adding each to your Bookmark list as you did with the IBM home page:

- **http://networth.galt.com/dreyfus/4134/** (Dreyfus Investments)

- **http://www.census.gov/** (U.S. Census Bureau)

- **http://www.w3.org/** (World Wide Web Consortium)

Now if you've added these Web pages to your Bookmark list, it should look like the one in Figure 6.3. (This also is an enlarged portion of a larger figure.)

As a comparison with the last lesson, take a look at your History list (select Go, View History) and you should see the same four Web sites. (If you didn't exit Netscape at the beginning of this lesson, your History still contains all the links you visited in the previous lessons.) Now exit Netscape once again, then restart it to see what happens to your History.

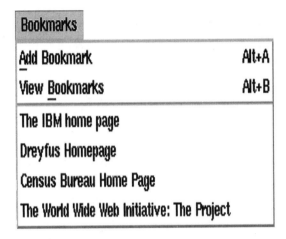

**Bookmarks**

| | |
|---|---|
| Add Bookmark | Alt+A |
| View Bookmarks | Alt+B |
| The IBM home page | |
| Dreyfus Homepage | |
| Census Bureau Home Page | |
| The World Wide Web Initiative: The Project | |

FIGURE 6.3    A Bookmark list with four Web pages added.

After restarting Netscape, you'll see that your History is again empty. Check out your Bookmarks, though, where you'll see the four Web pages you added are still on your list. Clicking any one of them takes you right back to that page.

To summarize the difference between Netscape's History and Bookmarks features:

- History accumulates a list of every Web page you visit *during a single Netscape session*; it disappears when you exit the program.

- Bookmarks are permanent markers you add, allowing you to retain a list of interesting Web pages *from one Netscape session to another*, so you can access them easily later.

# HISTORY, BOOKMARKS, AND CACHING

In a previous lesson, I mentioned Netscape's Cache feature. You might be unclear on the relationship between History and Bookmarks on the one hand, and Cache on the other. After all, they all seem to have something to do with keeping records of where you've been on the Web.

 **Check Your Stash**   As you access Web pages, Netscape quietly squirrels away copies of them on your local disk. If you use History, Bookmarks, or the Back/ Forward buttons to revisit a page, Netscape looks in its cache of pages to see if there's a copy. If there is, it'll reload that page from your local disk rather than retrieve it all over again across the Internet. Caching works also with Netscape's Open button, since Netscape pretty much always checks its cache first thing when a page is specified.

Caching speeds up your revisiting of Web pages but can result in getting out-of-date versions of frequently updated pages, such as What's New pages. How long these pages remain in your cache between updates depends on your available disk space and on some advanced Netscape Preference settings, which you'll learn about in Lesson 24. In the meantime, if you think a page may have been updated, just hit Reload to make sure you get the latest version.

# EXPLORE YOUR BOOKMARKS

As with most of the other lessons in this book, this one has introduced several potentially interesting Web pages. While they were introduced as examples to help you get started with Bookmarks, before you go on to the next lesson, you may want to take some time to explore these pages. At the very least, you'll discover whether you want to keep any or all of them on your Bookmark list.

In this lesson, you learned about Bookmarks—how to set them and how to use them. In the next lesson you will learn how to edit and delete your Bookmarks.

# EDITING AND DELETING BOOKMARKS

*In this lesson, you will learn how to edit and delete Bookmarks from your list of Web pages.*

In the previous lesson, you learned to add Web pages you've visited to your Bookmark list. Unlike the History list, the Bookmark listing is a permanent record, remaining from session to session.

## EDITING BOOKMARKS

The information Netscape gathers about a Web page when you place a Bookmark is pretty terse. Just the page's URL and Title, along with the date you created the Bookmark, gets saved. Web page authors frequently give poor titles to their pages, or worse, use generic ones like *So-and-So Home Page.* When you set a Bookmark, Netscape just grabs this information off the page and stores it. As a result, a Bookmark you place today may or may not be a useful Bookmark a few weeks—or months—from now.

Netscape lets you edit your Bookmark lists to make their titles more descriptive and to add annotations—your own notes to yourself about Web pages you like. Let's enter a new URL, add it to your Bookmark list, and then edit the Bookmark listing to illustrate.

Open Location and jump to the following Web page:

**http://www.disney.com/**

You can probably guess this is the Walt Disney home page, but may not realize until you visit that it's specifically used to showcase Disney's *movies.* Take a look at Figure 7.1.

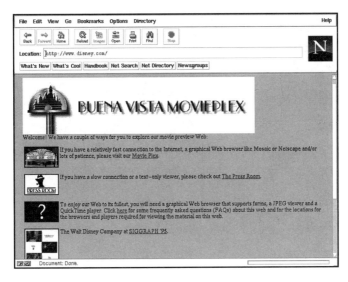

**FIGURE 7.1**    The Buena Vista MoviePlex.

*Buena Vista MoviePlex* is not particularly informative as a title. Add this page to your Bookmark list. (Select Bookmark, Add Bookmark.) You want to change the title of this Bookmark. To do so, select Bookmark, View Bookmarks. Figure 7.2 shows the View Bookmarks dialog box.

**Don't Touch that Mouse**    There are power-user keystroke combinations displayed on the Bookmark menu for both Add and View. Pressing these combinations allows you to open these functions without taking your hands from the keyboard. Be aware, though, these commands work silently, and you won't see anything on-screen to indicate their success until you view your Bookmark list again. UNIX is like that: commands that are successful often don't tell you so, and new users find this a bit disconcerting.

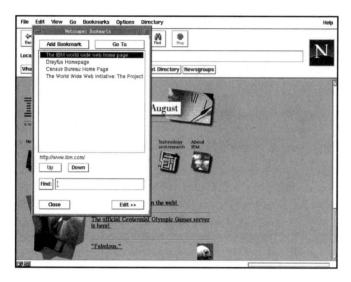

FIGURE 7.2   The View Bookmarks dialog box.

Now, click Edit >> (lower right). This expands the View Book-marks dialog box to the right, creating the Bookmark Editing dialog box (see Figure 7.3).

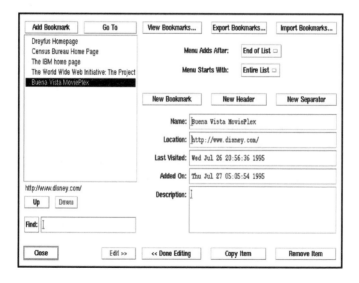

FIGURE 7.3   The Bookmark Editing dialog box.

This is quite a busy window, as you can see, so let's break it down. Compare it to Figure 7.2, and you'll see the left-hand side is the same dialog box you just left. You can see this more clearly if you click << Done Editing and then click Edit >> again.

The right side of the window is divided into several main areas. For this lesson, concentrate on the lower right-hand quarter, where you'll see boxes labeled Name, Location, and so on. (We'll return to this dialog box in Lesson 8 and cover its other functions.)

Your initial objective was to change the title of this Bookmark to make it more descriptive. To do this:

1. Move your mouse cursor to the Name box.

2. Edit this field using normal X Windows mouse selection. Click and drag to highlight Buena Vista MoviePlex, and then press your Delete key. (You could have also just used the Delete or Backspace key repeatedly, of course.)

3. Type in your new title, such as Disney Movie Home Page.

While you're here, you might want to enter some notes about the page to serve as a reminder next time you look at your Bookmark list. Place the cursor in the Description box and enter a sentence or two describing the home page. Your description can be up to 500 characters.

 **TIP**    **Cut-and-Paste**   You have all your normal X Windows editing capabilities here—such as backspace, delete, cut-and-paste and so on— with which to edit the description to your satisfaction.

To save your changes, select Close. If you want to edit another Bookmark, select it instead; Netscape will save the one on which you were working. To check to see that your change was made, select Bookmarks again, where you'll see that your list now includes Disney Movie Home Page. See Figure 7.4.

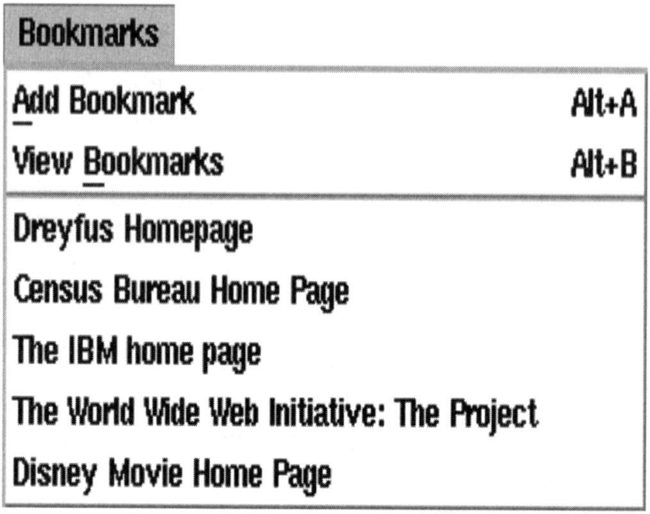

| Bookmarks | |
|---|---|
| **Add Bookmark** | Alt+A |
| **View Bookmarks** | Alt+B |
| Dreyfus Homepage | |
| Census Bureau Home Page | |
| The IBM home page | |
| The World Wide Web Initiative: The Project | |
| Disney Movie Home Page | |

FIGURE 7.4    The modified Bookmark list.

To view the description you entered, you must select View Bookmarks and then click Edit >>.

## DELETING BOOKMARKS

In the last two lessons, you added several Web pages to your Bookmark list. You're probably not interested in keeping all (or even any) of them on your personal Bookmark list. If so, delete them. It's simple:

1. Pull down Bookmarks, and then select View Bookmarks (or press Alt+B).

2. Click Disney Movie Home Page.

3. Click Edit >>.

4. Click Remove Item (on the lower right).

5. Select Close to save the changes to your Bookmark list.

Reopen the Bookmark list and you'll see the listing for the *Disney Movie Home Page* is gone. All references to this page have been removed from your Bookmark list, including the description you entered earlier.

Although it's tempting to practice deleting Bookmarks with any of the examples you've added in the last two lessons, keep them for one lesson longer—you'll need them.

In this lesson, you learned to edit and delete Bookmark listings. This can help you clean up a lengthy list of Bookmarks, but won't make it easier to use if it's any longer than a few items. As your Bookmark list grows, you'll want to be able to arrange it in a logical way. In the next lesson you'll learn to organize your Bookmark list.

# ORGANIZING YOUR BOOKMARKS

*In this lesson, you will learn how to organize your Bookmarks.*

Once you start using Netscape on a regular basis, it won't take long before your Bookmark list gets unmanageable. Searching through a list of a hundred Bookmarks for that particular page is no fun. Computers are supposed to make life easier, not harder, right? Fortunately, Netscape has a couple of ways to organize your list.

## REARRANGING YOUR BOOKMARK LIST

The simplest reorganization is to rearrange the order. Reopen the Bookmark listing you've built in the last two lessons (Select Bookmarks, View Bookmarks). It should look like Figure 8.1.

Let's move the IBM home page to the top. Highlight it; then click Up. As you can see, the entry moves up one spot on the list; click Up again to move it to the top. Similarly, move items down the list with the Down button.

**The Down (or Up) Button Doesn't Work** If you've highlighted an item that's already at the bottom of the list, the Down button is grayed out, indicating you can't move something at the bottom any further down. Up works the same way.

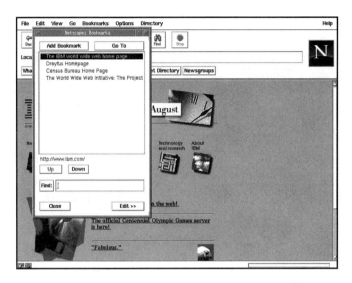

FIGURE 8.1 A Bookmark list.

# CREATING BOOKMARK LIST SUBMENUS

Although moving Bookmarks up and down will help you organize your list, you'll soon want a better way. Figure 8.2 shows an unorganized Bookmark list. As you can see, this is a random list of Bookmarks acquired from various browsing sessions. Figure 8.3 shows the same list reorganized.

As you can see, instead of the long list of Bookmarks in Figure 8.2, this is a very short one, with only four items showing. But, there's something new here: little triangles appear at the right side of each entry, pointing to the right. You probably recognize this standard X Windows trick from other UNIX programs you use, indicating there's another menu available. I've cheated in Figure 8.3 by dragging down the menu to one of the items and clicking to open a submenu, showing a list of Bookmarks.

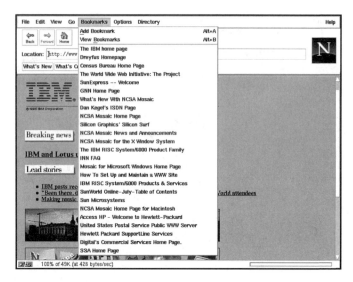

**FIGURE 8.2**   An unorganized Bookmark list.

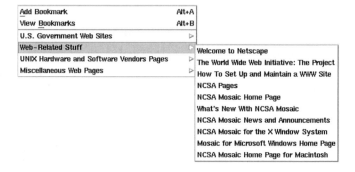

**FIGURE 8.3**   An organized Bookmark list.

Let's do a similar transformation with your Bookmarks. You don't
have the same list of Bookmarks, so first generate one. Jump to
each of these Web sites and set a Bookmark for each:

> **http://www.umkc.edu/**
>
> **http://www.udel.edu/**
>
> **http://www.ukans.edu/**

http://www.ucla.edu/

http://www.harvard.edu/

Obviously, these are all university pages. Let's create a University Web Pages submenu and put these into it. Select Bookmarks, View Bookmarks to open your Bookmark list. Click Edit >> to expand the Bookmark dialog box. Figure 8.4 shows the example Bookmark list from above, with the five new Bookmarks added at the bottom.

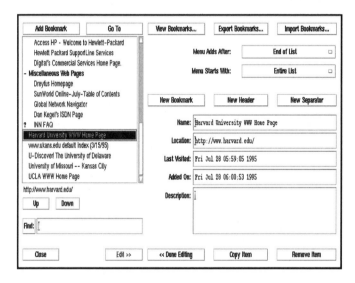

**FIGURE 8.4**   The Bookmark dialog box with university pages.

Highlight the Harvard item and select New Header. A new listing appears below the listing for Harvard, called - New Header (see Figure 8.5). Note the hyphen as the first character of this new item; you'll see another entry with it a few lines up on Figure 8.5 (Miscellaneous Web Pages).

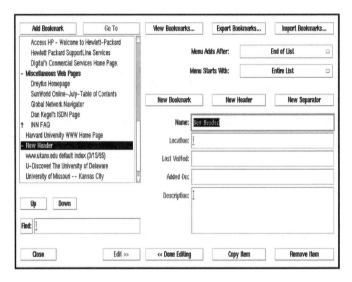

**FIGURE 8.5**    The **- New Header** listing.

**- New Header** is highlighted in the Name box, so press your Delete key to get rid of the text, and then insert (as you learned in Lesson 7) **University Web Pages**.

Since the new University Web Pages Bookmark is *above* the Harvard listing, highlight Harvard, and then click Down to place it under the new submenu. Notice the Harvard listing is now indented and part of the University Web Pages submenu.

Highlight each of the other university listings and use Up and/or Down to move them into the submenu, placing them in any order you want. Figure 8.6 shows the final result.

As Figure 8.6 shows, Bookmark submenu titles appear in boldface with a preceding hyphen. Submenu items are indented. It's only possible to create one submenu level, so you can't nest submenus within other submenus. Nonetheless, you'll agree that this is a great way to clean up your Bookmark list. Figure 8.7 shows the added University Web Pages submenu.

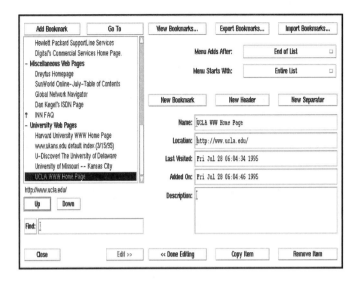

**FIGURE 8.6** The University Web Pages submenu.

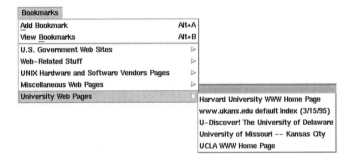

**FIGURE 8.7** Bookmarks with the University Web Pages submenu.

In this lesson, you learned how to organize your rambling list of Web site Bookmarks into a coherent, efficient listing using submenus. In the next lesson you will learn how to find Web pages using a keyword search.

# SEARCHING FOR WEB SITES BY KEYWORDS

*In this lesson, you will learn how to search for Web pages by keyword.*

With more than a million World Wide Web sites in existence and new ones appearing daily, you may have begun to wonder how (or if) anyone keeps track of them. How can you locate any Web pages that might be of interest to you?

## SEARCH ENGINES

Several Web search engines exist that help with these problems. Search engines are interactive Web pages that allow you to enter search criteria into a fill-in form, and then pass the criteria off to powerful computer programs that can quickly search vast indices of Web data. Usually, search engines return the information they find to your Netscape screen, with hyperlinks pointing to the data.

Access to several search engines is built into Netscape. Click Net Search (Netscape Directory Buttons, third button from the right). This opens Netscape's Internet Search page, shown in Figure 9.1.

Netscape's Internet Search Page (there's a good deal more to the page than what's shown in Figure 9.1) features three main methods of searching for information on the Web. We'll look at two of them in this lesson. You may want to look at the other hyperlinks on this page later on.

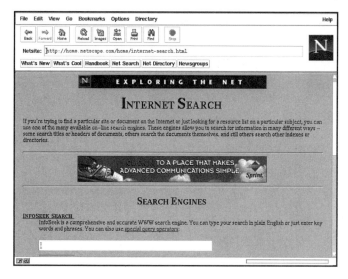

**FIGURE 9.1** The Netscape Internet Search page.

# INFOSEEK

InfoSeek is a commercial search-and-retrieval service. You can try out InfoSeek for a month at no cost. (Full InfoSeek service costs $9.95 a month, plus a dime per search after the first 100.) You can also try out InfoSeek directly from the Netscape Internet Search page at no cost. Just fill in the box with one or more words you'd like to search for, and then click Run Query. Try entering **star trek**. (Of course, you can enter any search string you want.) Figure 9.2 shows something like what you'll get—although the Web will have changed by the time you read this, and your results may look different in some way.

The results page from InfoSeek, as you can see, contains both explanatory text and several hyperlinks to other Web pages. You can click them to continue your search, but first note some things about the Results page:

- You can initiate a new search by clicking the blue New Search button.

- There's a link labeled helpful tips.

- You're limited to 10 hits with this demonstration search.

 **Search String** InfoSeek and other search engines do searches based on strings of text you specify. The example you just tried—*star trek*—is seen as two literal strings of characters s-t-a-r and t-r-e-k. Results will be returned on documents containing one word and not the other, as well as those with both. Search engines also allow you to use what are called Boolean searches to refine your searches. These are searches in which you ask for searches based on multiple search strings. A Boolean search for "star" *and* "trek" ensures the returns will contain both words.

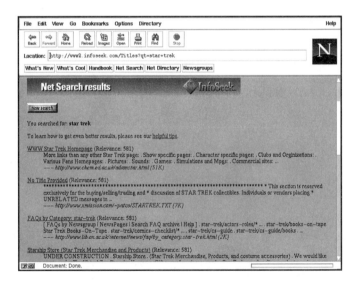

**FIGURE 9.2**   The InfoSeek Net Search results page.

**Hits**   The number of Web pages found as a result of your search. The 10-hit limit in InfoSeek prevents the display of any more hits that might have been found.

# LYCOS

Further down the Netscape Internet Search page, you'll find Lycos, the Catalog of the Internet. This search engine, originally set up by folks at Carnegie Mellon University in Pittsburgh, PA, is one of the most widely used Internet search engines. Lycos is a World Wide Web robot that searches out URLs automatically. You'll learn about Web robots and other Web crawlers a little later in this lesson. Let's look at using Lycos first.

Lycos searches a database with over six million Web pages. Lycos is updated about every 10 days, but also allows you to both submit URLs for inclusion and ask that certain listed URLs be deleted. Figure 9.3 shows the Lycos home page.

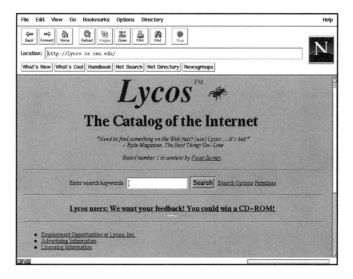

FIGURE 9.3   The Lycos home page.

Let's try our *star trek* search on Lycos. Click Search Options to
open a fill-in form for your search, shown in Figure 9.4. (There's a
simple search box on the Lycos home page, as shown in Figure
9.3, but the fill-in form has more flexibility in setting up your
searches.)

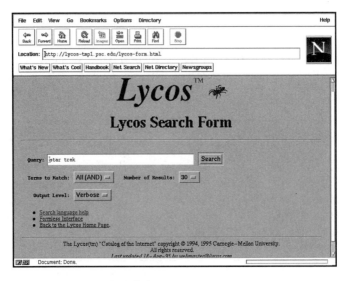

FIGURE 9.4   Lycos' search form.

In this form, you'll find not only a box into which you can type
your search words but also some other ways to set up your search.
Lycos' online help (click Search language help) explains the form,
as well as telling you how to tailor your search queries.

Notice the pull-down menu, with which you select the maximum
number of hits you want returned (the default is 10). Let's up this
number to 30 for your search. Next, use the pull-down menu
labeled Any(OR) to select Any(AND), and then enter **star trek** in
the Query box.

**Any(OR)**  Lycos uses this menu to allow you to limit your search to only Web pages containing both the words *star* and *trek*. Otherwise, your search would turn up thousands of Web pages containing *star* and other thousands containing *trek*, along with those containing both. See the Lycos' online help for details.

Figures 9.5 and 9.6 show overlapping views of your search results. Even so, as the scroll bar in the Netscape display indicates, the page is much longer than shown here.

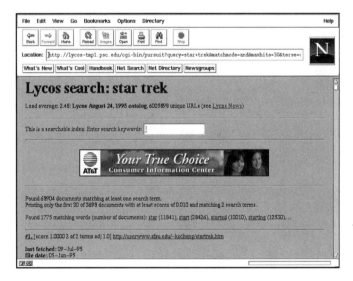

**FIGURE 9.5**   Lycos search results (Screen 1).

These search results are quite busy-looking; let's take them apart and look at the pieces individually so you'll have a better overall picture. First, you see there's yet another search terms box you can fill in to do additional keyword searches. Also, the form tells you how many actual hits Lycos found on your search terms (68,904 containing either *star* or *trek*, and 3,698 containing both).

Besides this general information, Lycos has also returned hyperlinks to the 30 Web pages with the highest relevance score. This
scoring is based on the *number* of occurrences of your search
terms within each located document, along with their *proximity* to
each other within each. Thus, in your search, documents with
multiple occurrences of both "star" and "trek" would rank high,
as would those in which the two words appear immediately adja-
cent to each other in the text. The highest possible score is 1.0.
Your hits are sorted with the highest score first.

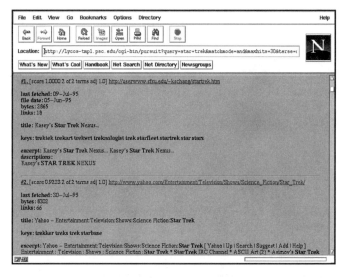

**FIGURE 9.6**   Lycos search results (Screen 2).

With respect to the actual hits, as you can see, you're not only
given a hyperlink that'll take you right to the Web page, but also
some summary information about each. All the way down at the
bottom of the search results, you'll find a hyperlink that'll show
you the next 30 hits.

The Lycos search technology was purchased by CMG Information
Services, Inc., in June 1995, but CMG's initial announcements
have indicated use of Lycos will remain free.

>
> **TIP** **Just in Case** You may want to add the Lycos search engine to your Netscape Bookmark list.

# Web Robots and Web Crawlers

You'll recall the characterization of Lycos (above) as a Web robot. Robots—also referred to as Web crawlers—are computer programs that automatically search the Internet for Web pages, using a variety of mechanisms, and then index the results for searching. The search mechanisms include, but are not limited to, these methods:

- Brute force attempts to connect using the Web's http protocol to every host the robot can locate using the Internet Domain Name Service

- Scanning Usenet news postings for URLs in article text

Netscape's Net Search button takes you to WebCrawler, where you'll find the now-familiar fill-in form interface to searching its database. (Because this service was recently bought out by America Online, you may see changes in it soon.) Other robots include the World Wide Web Worm, **http://www.cs,colorado.edu/home/mcbryan/WWWW.html**; EINet Galaxy, **http://galaxy.einet.net/galaxy.html**; and the brand-new Harvest, **http://harvest.cs.colorado.edu/**.

You may be wondering by now if anyone's gathered all these search engines into once place. If so, you'll want to try out CUSI, the Configurable Unified Search Interface, accessible on the Netscape Net Search page. Here, you'll find a single fill-in-form interface to a number of search engines.

In this lesson, you learned how to search for Web pages by keywords. Keyword searches, however, aren't the only way to locate Web pages. In the next lesson you will learn how to search more broadly for Web pages.

# 10 SEARCHING FOR WEB PAGES BY SUBJECT

*In this lesson, you will learn how to search for Web pages by subject.*

In Lesson 9, you learned how to use a couple of Web search engines to locate Web pages using keyword search. You may want a broader method of searching, say, by subject. The most common such tool is called Yahoo.

## YAHOO

Yahoo was developed at Stanford University but is now a commercial venture. Yahoo searches remain free, however. In addition to its listing by subject, Yahoo also has a keyword-search engine. I'll cover both.

Yahoo's database is organized into broad subjects, ranging from Art to Society and Culture. To access Yahoo, click the Netscape Net Directory. Figure 10.1 shows the Yahoo Major subject areas.

## SEARCHING YAHOO BY SUBJECT

You can start a Yahoo search right from this page by selecting one of the subject hyperlinks, or you can access the Yahoo home page by clicking YAHOO DIRECTORY (**http://www.yahoo.com/**).

Let's continue using *star trek* in our search examples. This time, however, we're using the phrase "star trek" as a *subject*, rather than just as a *string of text* for which to search.

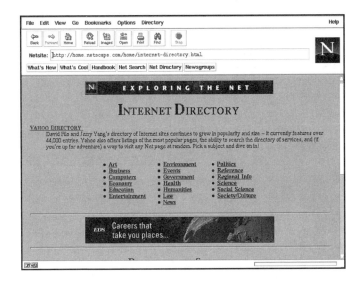

**FIGURE 10.1**    The Netscape Internet Directory.

Taking a look at the list of Yahoo subject areas, it's a good bet your search will start with Entertainment. This brings up Yahoo's main Entertainment page, which is also divided into Subject areas, each one of which is a hyperlink. Scroll down the list to look for a likely next jump. How about Television?

Clicking Television brings up another list of Subjects. (By now, you're getting the basic idea of Yahoo.) On this list, Shows looks like the next likely jump. Here again, you find a list of subjects as you continue to narrow down your search. Select Science Fiction.

There's an actual Star Trek entry on the Science Fiction list. Select this hyperlink to open the Web page shown in Figure 10.2.

Here at last is your destination, with real-live hyperlinks on Star Trek subjects. If you think this process was tedious, remember Lesson 9, where your Lycos search on the text string *star trek* turned up nearly 4,000 hits. You got here with five mouse clicks.

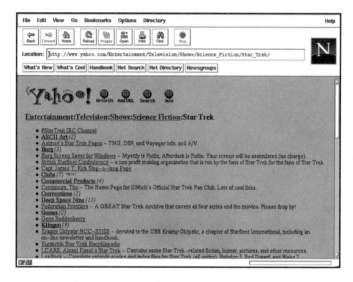

FIGURE 10.2    Yahoo's Entertainment:Television:Shows:Science Fiction:Star Trek page.

## SEARCHING YAHOO BY KEYWORD

As mentioned earlier, Yahoo also has a keyword search feature to search its database. It works much like Lycos. You may have noticed most Yahoo pages have a standard set of hyperlinks at the top:

**[Yahoo | Up | Search | Suggest | Add | Help]**

As you can see, there's a Search item here. Let's try it out, but first click Yahoo to return to Yahoo's home page, shown in Figure 10.3, so your search is initiated at the top level.

To start your keyword search, click Options, which brings up Yahoo's Search page, shown in Figure 10.4. (The search box on the home page doesn't allow you any flexibility in setting up your search.) Like the Lycos search page, this one is a fill-in form, but it's considerably more user friendly. Besides the box in which to enter keywords (and the advertisement), there are several buttons to set criteria for your search. Notice you can specify your searches include (or exclude) Web page titles, URLs, and any

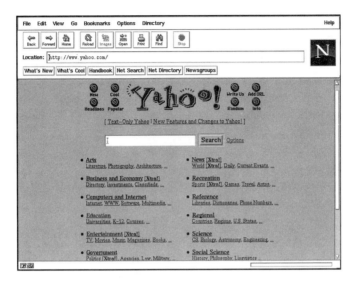

FIGURE 10.3    The Yahoo home page.

author comments in the HTML source document. You can also specify how you want your search string to be treated. Finally, you can limit the number of hits.

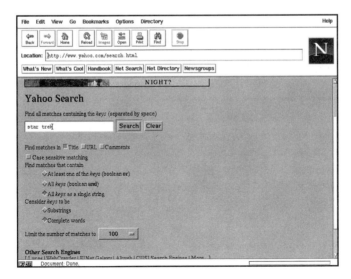

FIGURE 10.4    The Yahoo Search page.

Notice in Figure 10.4 the search criteria are already filled in, with some small changes in the default search criteria. See Figure 10.5 for the results of your search.

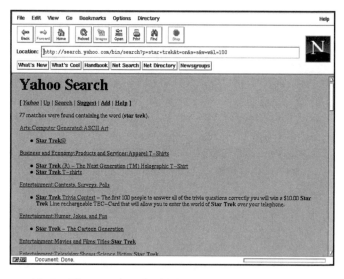

FIGURE 10.5   The results of a Yahoo keyword search.

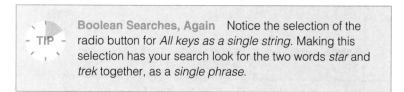

**Boolean Searches, Again**   Notice the selection of the radio button for *All keys as a single string*. Making this selection has your search look for the two words *star* and *trek* together, as a *single phrase*.

Yahoo's keyword search has a nice feature, which you'll notice in Figure 10.5. In addition to giving you the expected series of hyperlinks pointing to Web pages containing your keywords, Yahoo also includes links to Yahoo *subject* pages containing the individual pages found. For example, you'll find announcement of a Star Trek Trivia Contest about two-thirds of the way down Figure 10.5. Just above is a link to the Entertainment:Contests, Surveys, Polls page.

You'll agree this extra feature in Yahoo's keyword search complements the Subject search. Used together, the two methods of searching can supercharge your Web searches.

## Which Is Best, Yahoo or Lycos?

Both Lycos and Yahoo have unique features that make them valuable search tools. As you use them, you'll learn how one is better than the other in some respects, but less valuable in others. As you use them, you'll get a feel for which is best for any given kind of search and which suits the way you like to work.

 **Other Subject-Oriented Searches?** You'll learn another method of doing subject-oriented searches with Gopher in Lesson 14. Gopher is a purely text-based system for information retrieval, but can help you locate information in libraries and other sources.

In this lesson, you learned how Netscape helps you use one of the most popular subject search tools on the Web—the Yahoo Directory. In the next lesson you will learn how to use Netscape to do geographical searches on the World Wide Web.

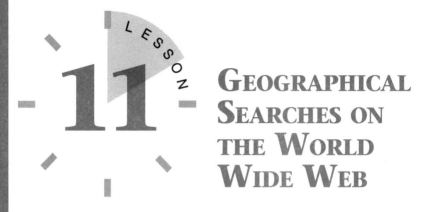

# GEOGRAPHICAL SEARCHES ON THE WORLD WIDE WEB

*In this lesson, you will learn how to search for Web servers by their geographical location, as well as a bit about getting tourist/travel information on the Web.*

In the previous two lessons, you learned to search for Web pages by keyword and by subject. Another way to locate Web servers is to search databases that are indexed by geographical location.

## GEOGRAPHICAL SERVERS

You may want to know if there are any Web servers in your area or your state, or even if there are Web servers in a given country of the world. Netscape has links to two geographical Web servers wired in. Both are accessible from Netscape's Internet Directory, the relevant portion of which is shown in Figure 11.1

### WORLD WIDE WEB SERVERS AT CERN

CERN is the European Laboratory for Particle Physics near Geneva. Birthplace of the World Wide Web, CERN has recently handed off all its Web-related activities to a new consortium, W3, which is now a major center of Web-related research and development. While you'll still see CERN's name on Web pages, as on the Netscape Internet Directory (accessible by clicking Net Directory), all CERN's former Web resources are now handled by W3.

From the Internet Directory, select WORLD WIDE WEB SERVERS. This will take you to the page shown in Figure 11.2.

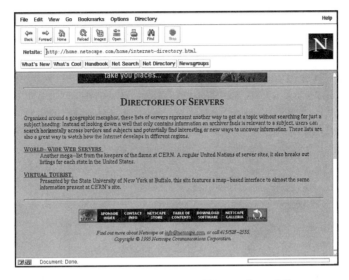

FIGURE 11.1    The Netscape Internet Directories of Servers.

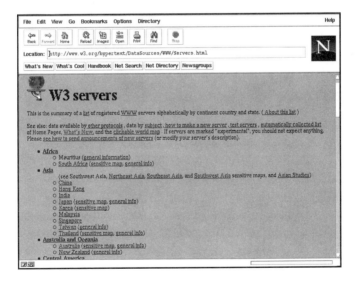

FIGURE 11.2    W3 servers.

Although this page is too large to show in a single figure, you can see that it's organized geographically, by continent and country. Each entry is a hyperlink.

Click a country. Depending on the country you select, you'll get different results. In some cases, you'll get a context-sensitive map; in others, a plain-text listing of Web server links. The map of Japan shown in Figure 11.3 is an example of the former. (This is a clickable image map, a subject you learned about in Lesson 5.) This map of Japan contains links to the Web servers in that country; just click one of the red dots.

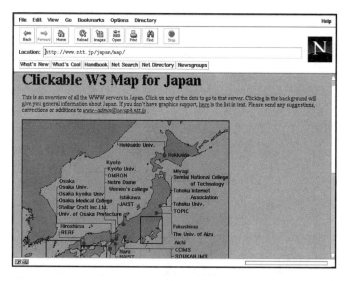

FIGURE 11.3    A clickable map of WWW servers in Japan.

Not all the links on the W3 Servers page have clickable image maps. For example, click Hong Kong to see the text listing for servers there.

Before you leave the W3 Servers page, note the hyperlinks near the top, which tell you about the service, including how entries can be added.

## VIRTUAL TOURIST

The University of Buffalo (New York) maintains another popular geographical Web server, The Virtual Tourist. The Virtual Tourist is also accessible from the Netscape Internet Directory page; its startup page is shown in Figure 11.4.

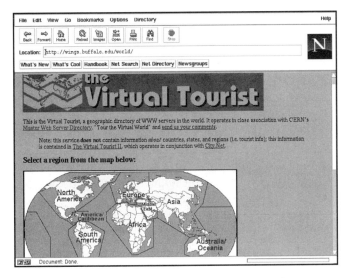

**FIGURE 11.4**   The Virtual Tourist.

You've probably already recognized the clickable image map on this page. Clicking a continent will jump you to a continent map. Clicking a country will jump you to a country map (or text listing if a map is not available). Depending on the country and concentration of Web servers in that country, your next jump will either be to a region (or state) in that country, with a clickable map or list of servers, or to a Web server in that country.

Since both the W3 and Virtual Tourist databases are in essence listings of the same Web servers, eventually you will jump to the same Web servers.

# TOURIST INFORMATION ON THE WEB

So far, this lesson has been concerned with Web servers that provide a geographical view of other Web servers. You might also want to use the Web to get tourist/travel information. There's no space for a great deal of detail here, but the maintainers of The Virtual Tourist have a second service, The Virtual Tourist II. Start out at the URL **http://wings.buffalo.edu/world/vt2/**, where you'll find a clickable map interface much like that in Figure 11.4.

Click your way progressively through continent, country, and region/state maps to find an area in which you're interested. You'll find the information and services accessible here vary widely from elaborate Web pages with graphical images containing hotel advertisements to plain-text listings of information. Your mileage may vary, depending on which trail of links you follow. Figure 11.5 shows a page about Chincoteague Island, VA, a resort on Virginia's Eastern Shore, located using The Virtual Tourist II.

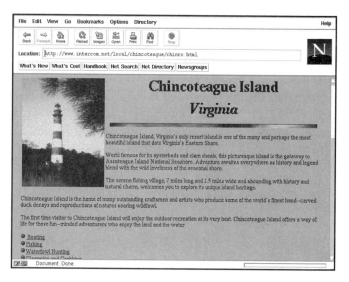

**FIGURE 11.5**   Chincoteague Island, Virginia.

You can find additional travel/tourism information with Yahoo (see Lesson 10), where you'll find a Travel subsection under the main Recreation section.

**TIP**    **Change Your Money**    Yahoo's Travel section features a currency exchange subsection you can use to pre-budget your overseas travel.

In this lesson, you learned how to use two popular databases to find servers located in geographical areas of the world. Also, you learned about getting tourist and travel information on the Web. In the next lesson you will learn how to search for people and their e-mail addresses on the Web.

# LESSON 12

# SEARCHING FOR PEOPLE ON THE INTERNET

*In this lesson, you will learn how to search for people—and their e-mail addresses—on the Internet.*

You can use any of the search engines we've covered in this book—Lycos, Yahoo, Gopher (see Lesson 14), and archie (see Lesson 15) to search for people's names on the Web. All these services allow searching on strings of text; of course, "Smith" or "Jones" is just a string of text. For example, Figure 12.1 shows the results of an InfoSeek (see Lesson 9) search for the text string "mickey mantle." You can do searches on other celebrity names as well, and find home pages for some of them, usually maintained by fans.

Netscape is plugged into several specific facilities for searching for people on the Internet, though. These people-search engines are still under development. Nonetheless, they can provide valuable help in locating people.

> **Call Them on the Phone** The example searches here use known names to illustrate successful searches. It's likely, though, that you'll find these people-search engines tedious and frustrating for several reasons. The available data is spotty. Many companies consider their corporate phonebook/e-mail directory proprietary and don't make it available. Other organizations live behind protective devices called Internet firewalls, which don't permit the probes sent out by people-search engines to pass. As a result, the best method of getting someone's e-mail address may well be the old-fashioned method of asking for it.

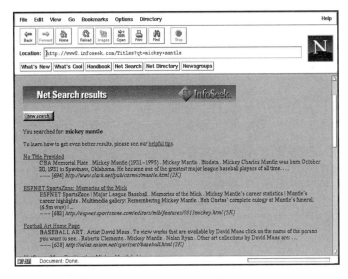

FIGURE 12.1  InfoSeek search results.

# NETFIND

Coordinated by programmers at the University of Colorado, Netfind is an evolving service that searches a variety of Internet resources likely to have user information in them. The list and description of the services are too long and complex for this book, but many feel Netfind is the best of the people-search engines.

You can access Netfind from Netscape's Directory menu; select Internet White Pages. This brings up People and Places, as shown in Figure 12.2.

Select NETFIND. This takes you to an introductory page on Netfind, on which you'll find a hyperlink that'll bring up a short fill-in form.

There's no helpful information on the form to give you an idea of what to enter. A good way to start is to type the last name of a person, along with some other identifying information. The latter can be a city or state, or a company name. If you know it, try the

Internet domain name (or part of one). Figure 12.3 shows a filled-in form.

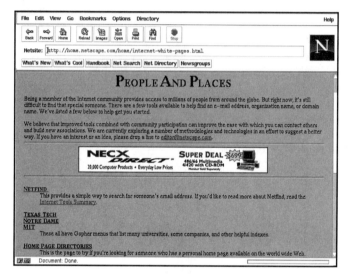

**Figure 12.2**   Netscape's People and Places page.

**Figure 12.3**   A Netfind fill-in form.

The result, shown in Figure 12.4, is a long list of e-mail domains at the University of Delaware. Because many organizations have a top-level e-mail domain, I've selected the fifth entry from the bottom in Figure 12.4—udel.edu—assuming all the others are subsidiary to this one. Selecting this entry gives the output in Figure 12.5.

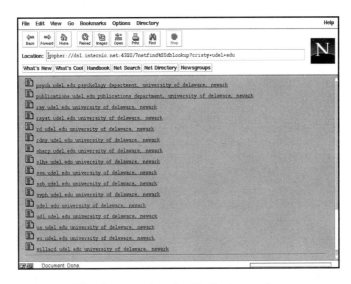

FIGURE 12.4    The first results of a Netfind search.

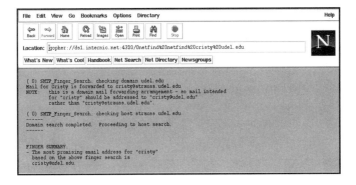

FIGURE 12.5    The final Netfind search results.

Unless you're familiar with the UNIX *finger* utility, you probably need a little interpretation of the information shown in Figure 12.5. Netfind uses many services to attempt to locate the names you request, one of which is finger. This service retrieves information about a given username on your local system, or (subject to some limitations) from remote systems over the Internet. The information finger retrieves normally consists of the user's real name and e-mail information, and may contain other information the user wants to be provided. Netfind retrieves this information and makes some interpretive efforts, as you can see by the recommended e-mail address in Figure 12.5.

**Domain Name Service**  Internet addressing is based on the Domain Name Service, or DNS. You've encountered domain names in URLs. DNS is a means of identifying computers on the Internet using an hierarchical naming system, with names like *www.netscape.com* and *udel.edu*. The latter is used in Figure 12.2 for the Netfind search, but, as you can see, the period in the domain name is replaced by a space.

## FOUR11 DIRECTORY SERVICE

Further down the Netscape People and Places Page, you'll find FOUR11 DIRECTORY SERVICE. While this is a commercial service, Four11 (pronounced *four-one-one*) is building its database by letting anyone register for free, as well as providing some simple search capabilities. You must register before you can use Four11's free services.

Four11 works with a fill-in form, shown already filled in with some search criteria in Figure 12.6. Note the use of the asterisk as a wild card in the First Name and City boxes. In the first case, the asterisk follows the letters *Dav*, limiting the search to first names beginning with those letters, such as *Dav*id, *Dav*is, *Dav*ina, and so on. In the second case, the asterisk means "any city." Figure 12.7 shows the results of the search.

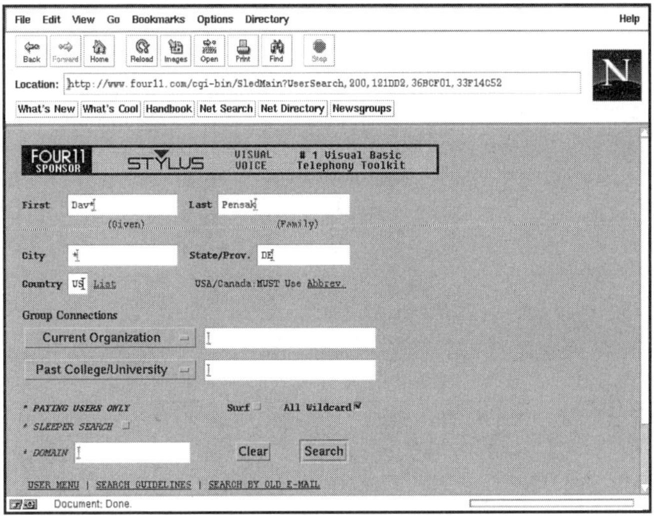

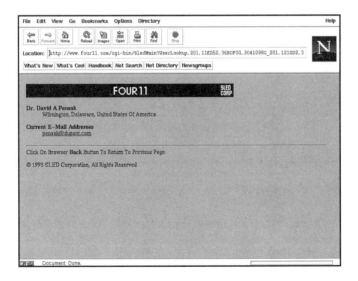

FIGURE 12.6   The Four11 search form.

FIGURE 12.7   The Four11 search results.

# INTERNIC SERVICES

As part of its contract for administering the Internet Network Information Center (InterNIC), AT&T makes several directory databases accessible on the Web. Netscape doesn't have the InterNIC service on any of its pull-down pages, but you can access **http://www/internic.net/ds/dspg01.html** directly. This service is similar to Netfind in that it uses Gopher services (see Lesson 14), but includes more than just name and address search capabilities. Figure 12.8 shows the InterNIC Directory and Database page.

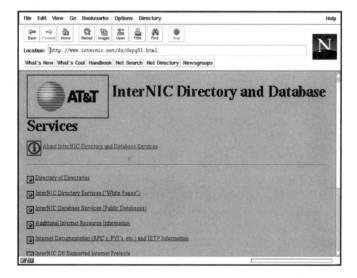

FIGURE 12.8    The InterNIC Directory and Database page.

In this lesson, you learned some ways to search for people on the Web. In the next lesson you will learn how to find interesting new Web sites.

# Searching for New and Interesting Web Sites

*In this lesson, you will learn how to keep up with the latest and the greatest sites on the World Wide Web.*

The World Wide Web is growing faster than anyone can imagine. How can you keep up with all the new and interesting Web pages? Early in the development of the Web, a tradition of gathering new Web resources into What's New pages arose.

## What's New

You've no doubt noticed Netscape's What's New Directory Button, first on the left. Selecting this jumps you to Netscape's What's New page, shown in overlapping Figures 13.1 and 13.2.

**What I Get Is Different**  The Netscape What's New page is updated regularly. The figures here show the page on July 26, 1995.

You'll notice that in the second figure there's a list of hyperlinks to Web pages/sites. This is a fairly short list, belying the statement above about the growth of the Web. Netscape keeps this list short, so as not to overwhelm you.

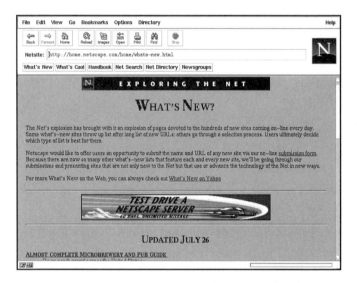

**FIGURE 13.1**   Netscape What's New page (part 1).

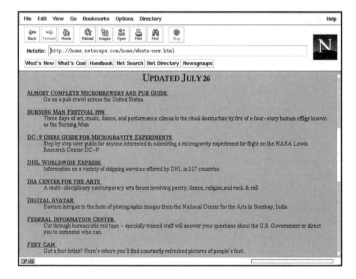

**FIGURE 13.2**   Netscape What's New page (part 2).

# WHAT'S NEW ON YAHOO

While you're looking at the Netscape What's New page, notice the hyperlink (refer to Figure 13.1) to the What's New on Yahoo page. (You learned to use Yahoo subject search in Lesson 10.) Figure 13.3 shows the first-level What's New page at Yahoo.

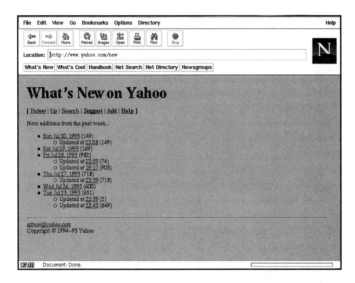

FIGURE 13.3    What's New on Yahoo page (summary).

Yahoo's What's New is substantially more extensive. As you can see, the first page has a list of hyperlinks, one for each day of the week. Jumping to any of them brings up a longer list, shown in Figure 13.4. The Yahoo listings are organized according to the major Yahoo subject areas. Yahoo's search feature is available here.

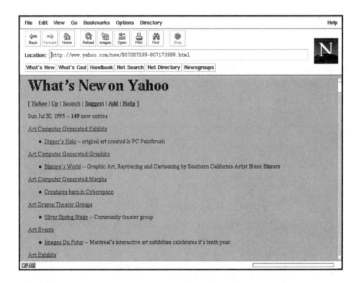

FIGURE 13.4    The What's New on Yahoo page (detail).

# NCSA WHAT'S NEW

Some people view Netscape and NCSA Mosaic as rivals. This is
more than a little silly, and the omission of a link to NCSA's
What's New page on the Netscape What's New page is, too. The
National Center for Supercomputing Applications is a major con-
tributor to the Web, not only because of Mosaic but also because
of its widely used NCSA Web server software.

NCSA maintains an extensive What's New, updated three times a
week; you'll want to access it frequently. Click Open and access
this URL (see Figure 13.5):

> **http://www.nsca.uiuc.edu/SDG/Software/Mosaic/
> Docs/whats-new.html**

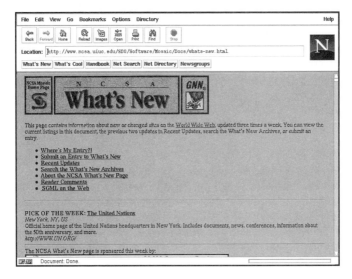

**FIGURE 13.5**    NCSA's What's New page.

# UPDATING WHAT'S NEW

You may be wondering how these pages get updated. For the most part, updating is done by users like you, who submit nominations for the list(s). Each of the What's New resources you've tried in this lesson allow submissions. All are based on fill-in forms. We'll look at just one of them here; the others are similar.

On the Netscape What's New page, you'll find a hyperlink submission form (refer to Figure 13.1). Figure 13.6 shows the form.

Fill in the blanks with the type of Web resource you'd like added, its URL, title, and someone to contact for additional information. Since Netscape keeps its page short and no one knows the criteria by which new entries are selected, there's a good chance yours won't show up. You'll probably want to add your announcement to the other What's New lists as well.

Most people who maintain Web pages are willing to accept submissions of new and interesting Web sites, especially if the new

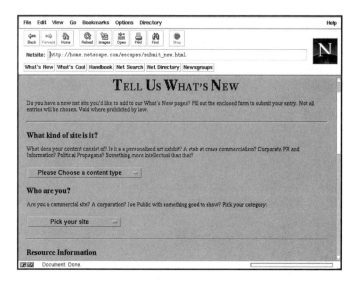

FIGURE 13.6    The Netscape What's New submission form.

sites fit into the site Webmaster's scheme of things. Often, you can simply send e-mail to the Webmaster, asking that your suggested link be added. Some Web sites actually allow you to add links yourself. See the URL **http://www.yahoo.com/Computers_and_Internet/World_Wide_Web/Announcement_Services/**.

**TIP**    **Start Your Own Web Page**    One way to let the Internet community know what you think is interesting is to put your own Web page up. The *10 Minute Guide to HTML* can get you started. Who knows? If you do a good enough job, your own site will show up on someone's list of new and interesting sites.

# NETSCAPE WHAT'S COOL

Even with these What's New listings, you may still have trouble finding Web resources interesting to you. Web pages range from the widely interesting, with spectacular graphical or other features, to the highly specialized. If there's a particular area of research or a hobby you're interested in, chances are good there's someone out there who has a page about it. Many people use Web pages as personal statements of some kind. Some of these personal home pages may be of interest, but you'll find others are self-indulgent and of interest primarily to the person who created them. After all, the Web is the world's largest vanity press: anyone can put anything he wants in a Web page.

How, then, do you find interesting Web resources? Recognizing that what's interesting to one person may be dull and boring—or even offensive—to another, the people at Netscape nonetheless attempt to keep a useful listing. Take a look at what you get when you click the What's Cool Directory Button, second from the left. Figure 13.7 shows this page.

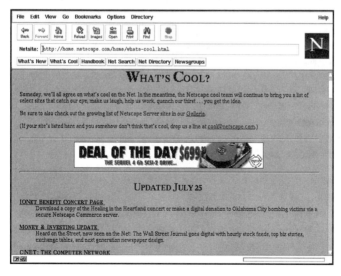

FIGURE 13.7    The Netscape What's Cool page.

As with What's New pages, this one is updated on a regular basis, so you'll want to visit often. Most of the people at Netscape who put together this list are quite young, and the selections made very much reflect the interests of young people. What's on this list may or may not suit your definition of "cool." If you'd like to comment on Netscape's What's Cool page, send e-mail to **cool@netscape.com**.

## OTHER WAYS OF SEARCHING FOR NEW AND INTERESTING WEB PAGES

Since the phrases *what's new* and *what's cool* are widely used on the World Wide Web, you may want to try searching for these text strings in the Web search engines I've described. Watch the Usenet newsgroups comp.infosystems.www.announce and comp.internet.net-happenings for announcements of new Web resources. (Lessons 16–17 deal with using Netscape to access Usenet newsgroups.)

You'll find a list of winners of Global Network Navigator's *Best of the Net* contest at URL **http://www.gnn.com/wic/best.toc.html**. GNN also publishes the online book *The Whole Internet Catalog*, at URL **http://www.gnn.com/wic/index.html**.

A large number of electronic magazines—e-zines—are accessible on the Web, many of which are *about* the Web and contain references to interesting Web sites. For a list, see the URL **http://www.yahoo.com/Entertainment/Magazines/Computers_and_Technology/**.

In this lesson, you learned how to use Netscape's What's New and What's Cool Directory Buttons to locate new and interesting Web sites. In the next lesson you will learn how to use Netscape to access Gopher services on the Internet.

# ACCESSING GOPHER SERVERS

*In this lesson, you will learn how to access Gopher servers using Netscape.*

Besides its graphical features, probably the most important thing about the World Wide Web—and about Netscape, too—is that you can use Web browsers to get to a lot of different Internet services. Over the next few lessons, you'll learn how to use Netscape to access these services—one service is Gopher, which is covered in this lesson.

## WHAT IS GOPHER?

So far, most of the places you've accessed in this book have been real World Wide Web pages, complete with graphics. You've seen in Lesson 12, though, the decidedly nongraphical Netfind. Netfind uses an Internet service called Gopher, one of several other Internet services Netscape supports.

The Gopher service arose at the University of Minnesota a couple of years *before* the Web. Gopher uses text-based menus arranged by subject—something like the Yahoo subject index. You start out at a top-level menu and work your way down a hierarchy of nested menus until you find the subject you're after. Once you find your subject, you're able to view text files on the subject and, in some cases, transfer files across the Internet to your own computer.

Besides the ability to read text files and download files to your own computer, some other Internet services are accessible via

Gopher. The Internet remote-login facility, Telnet, is sometimes available. Telnet allows you to log in to a remote computer system where you have an account and use your keyboard and screen as a remote terminal. Once logged in via Telnet, you can access almost any service available on the remote computer, just as if you were sitting at it.

Many Gopher menus have entries that take you to other Gopher servers. This is much like the Web's hyperlink capability; select a Gopher menu item and you'll jump to another Gopher server in some other location, where you'll get yet another menu.

## GOPHER AND NETSCAPE

The original Web developers (at CERN and NCSA) built support for Gopher services into the Web. The idea was to provide a single interface to several Internet services. All Web browsers, including Netscape, include Gopher support (as well as support for other Internet services).

You can use Netscape to explore gopherspace, the inter-connection of Gopher servers on the Internet. Figure 14.1 shows a Gopher menu, as accessed with Netscape; its URL is **gopher:// gopher.micro.umn.edu/**.

Although Gopher is a purely text-based service, you can see Netscape has dressed this menu up with some icons. In Figure 14.1, you see two different icons: a file folder, representing a Go-pher sub-menu, and a Question Mark, representing a searchable index.

Now you're connected to this Gopher server, try selecting a few items. The icons Netscape added to this menu don't do anything, so click Fun & Games to open a new menu. Next select Movies to jump to the menu shown in Figure 14.2.

Represents a sub-menu

Represents a searchable index

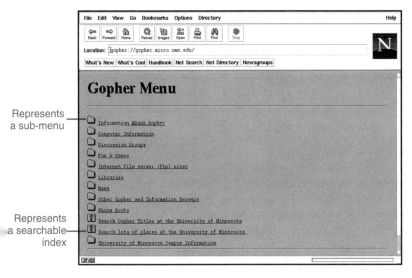

**FIGURE 14.1**   A typical Gopher menu.

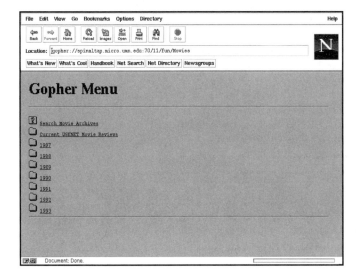

**FIGURE 14.2**   The Gopher Movie Review menu.

Clicking the search hyperlink brings up a fill-in form. Type kevin costner and press Enter. Figure 14.3 shows the results of your search.

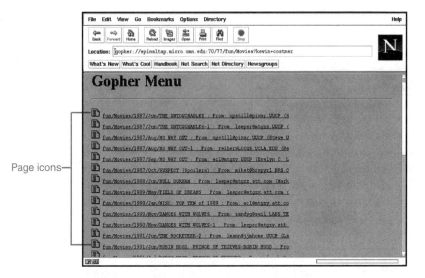

FIGURE 14.3    Results of a Gopher search.

Here, you'll see one more of the icons Netscape uses to dress up Gopher menus. In this case, the page icon (it has a folded-down corner) represents a text document you can view on-screen. Click any of the listed items to read about *Bull Durham*, *Field of Dreams*, or another movie.

Once you've finished reading, click Back to return to the listing shown in Figure 14.3. Notice there are some listings that aren't really reviews of a specific Kevin Costner movie. Open one of them and use Netscape Find (Edit, Find) to search for Kevin's name in the text.

# LOCATING GOPHER SERVERS USING VERONICA

As with Web services, you'll want to know how to search for useful Gopher services. You can use several search facilities to access Gopher indices. The most popular of these is Veronica.

**Veronica Is an Acronym** It stands for Very Easy ROdent-oriented Net-wide Index of Computerized Archives. This mouthful is an Internet play on words. A widely used service for searching FTP sites is named *archie* (Lesson 15). There's a comic book character named Archie; his girlfriend: Veronica.

# ACCESSING AND SEARCHING WITH VERONICA

To access Veronica, open the following URL (see Figure 14.4):

**gopher://veronica.scs.unr.edu/11/veronica**

**Nothing Happens** This is a popular and busy server, and you may not always connect to it. If this happens, wait a few minutes and try again.

There are a lot of items on the menu in Figure 14.4, but let's try a simple one. Select the Simplified veronica: Find Gopher MENUS only. This will take you to a fill-in form. Enter the keyword baseball. Figure 14.5 shows the results of this search.

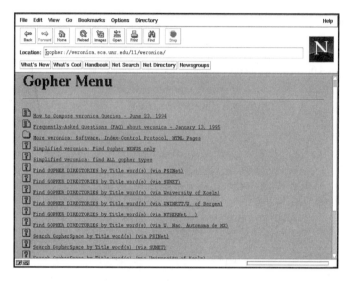

FIGURE 14.4    Veronica.

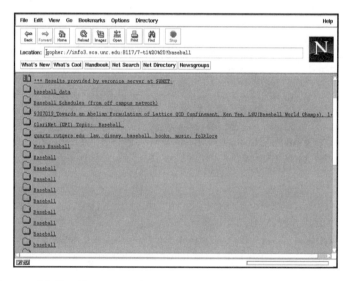

FIGURE 14.5    Query results.

# WHY THE NAME "GOPHER?"

Gopher is a multi-level play on words. First, as noted above, Gopher was created at the University of Minnesota. Minnesota's state animal is the gopher, and the *Golden Gopher* is the mascot of the university's athletic teams. Second, as you've learned, the service allows you to dig (like a gopher?) through layer upon layer of menus to find what you're looking for. Finally, the old gopher pun "go-fer" certainly comes into play.

In this lesson, you learned how to use Netscape to access and search Gopher servers and to use Veronica to search gopherspace. In the next lesson you will learn how to use Netscape to access FTP servers.

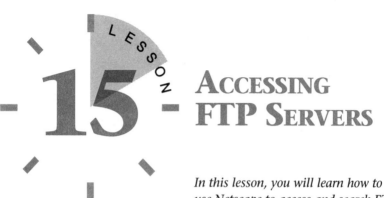

# ACCESSING FTP SERVERS

*In this lesson, you will learn how to use Netscape to access and search FTP servers on the Internet.*

In the last lesson, you learned about an Internet service called Gopher. Just as Netscape accesses Gopher, so can it get to other Internet services, such as FTP services—which you'll learn about in this lesson.

## WHAT IS FTP?

The Internet file transfer protocol (FTP) service is one of its oldest. As the name implies, FTP is used to transfer files over the Internet.

**Protocol** Math equations consist of symbols from a universally agreed-to set of symbols. New symbols are not allowed and the rules for using them are very specific. Network protocols work the same way. Like mathematicians, computer programs use a specific, agreed-to set of symbols to ensure precise communications.

The FTP protocol pre-dates the World Wide Web, and there have long been many uses of it. Computer vendors maintain servers so customers can download software updates. Your company may run an FTP server from which you can get company documents, such as operating procedures or employee benefit information. You might use FTP to share data with colleagues so you can work on a project together. Finally, there's a vast amount of free software available on the Internet for downloading using FTP.

Experienced UNIX users find the old-fashioned command-line interface to FTP quick and easy to use. More recently developed Internet services, like Gopher and the World Wide Web, have support for FTP built in, allowing access to existing FTP archives through new interfaces.

**Download**  To copy a file to your computer from another over the network or the Internet.

You might also know about *anonymous* FTP servers, which are like computer bulletin board systems (BBS). Like BBSs, anonymous FTP servers allow pretty much anyone to download files from them.

## ACCESSING FTP SERVERS WITH NETSCAPE

As it knows about Gopher, Netscape also knows about FTP, and you can use it to access anonymous FTP servers. Let's use Netscape to check on the latest release of Netscape and, if necessary, update your copy. First, pull down the Netscape Help menu and select About Netscape to get the version number of your copy of Netscape.

Click Open and enter the URL **ftp://ftp.netscape.com**. This takes you to Netscape's anonymous FTP server (see Figure 15.1).

Like Gopher, FTP is a nongraphical service. As with Gopher, though, Netscape dresses up FTP server listings with icons. As you see, each entry in the top-level directory listing has a file folder icon, indicating each is a subdirectory of the top-level directory.

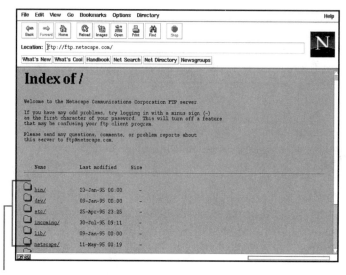

File folder icons

**Figure 15.1**    Netscape's FTP server.

# Navigating Through an FTP Server

Clicking a subdirectory takes you to that subdirectory. Let's go to the netscape subdirectory. Since you've descended a step in the hierarchy, you'll notice a hyperlink, Parent directory. Any time you need to move back upward in the directory tree, use this link. Since you're using UNIX Netscape, select the unix subdirectory. Figure 15.2 shows a listing of the files in the unix subdirectory.

There are a couple of things to notice here. First, note the several icons, one of which you haven't seen before. It looks something like a piece of paper, but it has little triangles pointing to both sides of it and looks crunched together. This indicates the files have been converted with the UNIX compress utility. (File compression makes them smaller, so they take less time to download.) See later in this lesson for more information about file compression.

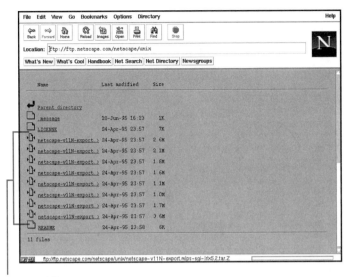

Compressed files

**FIGURE 15.2**   The Netscape FTP server's unix subdirectory.

Second, you'll notice the filenames all seem to be the same: netscape-v11N-export. What's happened here is the filenames are too long to be displayed, so they're truncated. The greater than symbols (>) confirm this. Figure 15.2 was shot with the mouse cursor resting on one of the hyperlinks; notice the full filename in the status information at the bottom of the screen. In this case, the figure shows the SGI version.

# DOWNLOADING A FILE FROM AN FTP SERVER

Let's assume you've determined there's a later version here. How do you get a copy from the Netscape server to your computer? With Netscape, this is as easy as pointing and clicking.

Move your mouse cursor down over the hyperlinks until you find the version for your UNIX system. Once you've found it, just click it. After a moment, Netscape pops up a dialog box, asking you for the name under which to save the to-be downloaded file. As Figure 15.3 shows, the filename defaults to the same name it has on the Netscape FTP server, but you can rename it and/or place it in a different directory on your system.

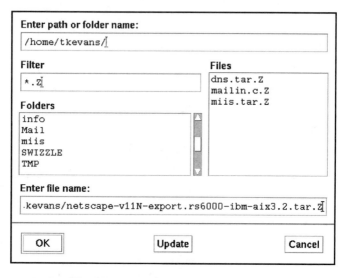

**Figure 15.3** The Netscape Save As dialog box.

This dialog box is pretty busy. First, on the left side of the window, labeled Folders, there's a scrollable list of the subdirectories of your current directory; choose one (by clicking it) to place your copy of Netscape there. Second, Netscape knows the filename ends in .Z and shows you the other files in your working directory that also end in .Z (to protect you from overwriting one with the same name). See the Files box.

Once you've decided what to name the file and where to place it, click OK to start the download. When the download is finished, you can install your new version of Netscape (see Appendix B).

# Compressed Files

Virtually all anonymous FTP servers store files in some kind of compressed format. Files with names ending in .Z have been processed with the UNIX compress command. Most UNIX systems have this utility, along with uncompress to reverse the conversion. More efficient file-compression packages are available, and a common one is the GNU gzip package. You can distinguish files which have been gzipped as their names end in .gz. If you don't have it, you'll want to get a copy.

To get gzip, use Netscape to access this URL:

>**ftp://prep.ai.mit.edu/pub/gnu/gzip-1.2.4.tar**

This will directly download the source code for gzip. You may need your system administrator's help in compiling and installing gzip.

**The Path Less Traveled**   In the previous paragraph, we used a *full path and filename* as an URL, going directly to the desired file, rather than to its parent directory.

# Locating Anonymous FTP Servers

We mentioned archie in Lesson 14. Worldwide, a series of archie servers, periodically search known anonymous FTP sites in their region and pool the results of their searches. You can access an archie server to search the combined databases.

As with FTP, archie predates the Web. It has a tortuous user interface, but, fortunately, Web people have built fill-in form interfaces. Information about archie is at URL **http:// web.nexor.co.uk/archie.html** (see Figure 15.4).

Select an archie server. (Picking one on your continent generally results in a faster search.) In the search request form (see Figure 15.5, which is the search form for ArchiePlex), type a text string; let's use gzip.

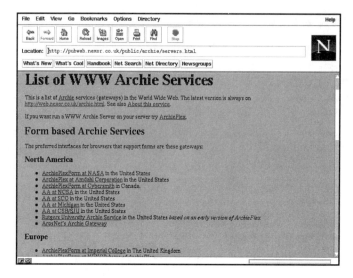

**FIGURE 15.4**    WWW Archie Services.

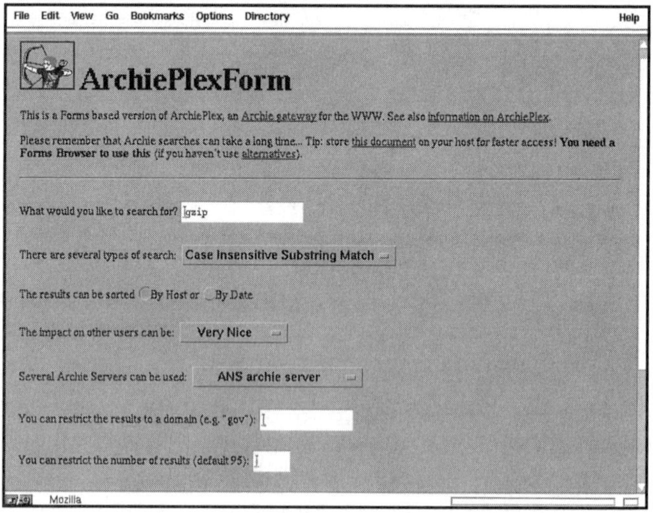

**FIGURE 15.5**    ArchiePlex request form.

There are options on this form to refine your search. The search
shown in Figure 15.5 accepts the defaults. You may want to
explore the options. Figure 15.6 shows the results of the search.

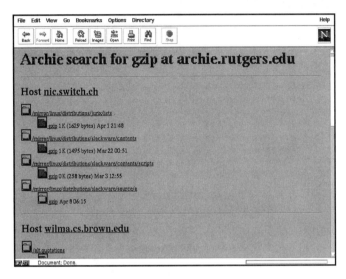

**FIGURE 15.6**   The results of archie search.

 **Get the Source**   If you expect to use archie services
**TIP**   frequently, you may want to ask your system administrator
to install the ArchiePlex software on your UNIX system.
Running it locally, rather than on a remote system, can
speed up searches. ArchiePlex is available at this URL:
ftp://pubweb.nexor.co.uk/public/archie/archieplex/
archieplex.tar.gz

In this lesson, you learned about using Netscape to search and
access FTP servers and how to download files from them. The
next lesson is about using Netscape to access Usenet newsgroups.

# 16 ACCESSING USENET NEWS AND NEWSGROUPS

*In this lesson, you will learn how to use Netscape to access Usenet newsgroups.*

Like Gopher and FTP (which you learned about in previous lessons), Usenet pre-dates the Web. It's a vast, moving, participatory, Mother-of-all-computer-bulletin-board-systems. You may already have used specialized newsreader programs, like rn, nn, or xrn (an X Windows version of rn) on your UNIX system. If so, some of this and the next lesson will be familiar.

## WHAT ARE USENET NEWSGROUPS?

Usenet—often called netnews, or just plain news—is broken into thousands of specialized newsgroups. Each is an electronic discussion group on a topic, ranging from aviation to zoology. comp.infosystems.www.browsers.x (about Web browsers for X Windows systems, like Netscape) and rec.outdoors.fishing are example newsgroups.

You'll find newsgroups minutely broken down. For example, in addition to the browsers newsgroup, there are about 15 other groups in the comp.infosystems.www hierarchy, all having one thing or another to do with the World Wide Web.

## CONFIGURING NETSCAPE FOR NEWS

Before you can use Netscape for news, you configure it. Select Options, Preferences, and then Mail and News. See the figure in Figure 16.1.

```
┌─────────────────────────────────────────────────────────────┐
│              ┌──────────────────────────────┐               │
│              │      Mail and News      ▭    │               │
│              └──────────────────────────────┘               │
│  ┌─ Mail ──────────────────────────────────────────────────┐│
│  │   Mail (SMTP) Server: │I                              │  ││
│  │         Your Name: │I                                 │  ││
│  │         Your Email: │I                                │  ││
│  │   Your Organization: │I                               │  ││
│  │     Signature File: │I                    │ Browse... │  ││
│  │   Send and Post: ◉ Allow 8-bit ○ MIME Compliant (Quoted Printable) ││
│  └─────────────────────────────────────────────────────────┘│
│  ┌─ News ──────────────────────────────────────────────────┐│
│  │   News (NNTP) Server: │I                              │  ││
│  │   News RC Directory: │                    │ Browse... │  ││
│  │         Show: │100    │ Articles at a Time            │  ││
│  └─────────────────────────────────────────────────────────┘│
│  ┌──────┐          ┌──────────┐          ┌──────────┐       │
│  │  OK  │          │  Cancel  │          │ Defaults │       │
│  └──────┘          └──────────┘          └──────────┘       │
└─────────────────────────────────────────────────────────────┘
```

**FIGURE 16.1**    The Mail and News preferences dialog box.

As you can see, there are a number of blanks to be filled in. Focus on the lower part of the box, labeled News; we'll cover Mail in Lesson 20. Here's what to enter:

1. In the News (NNTP) Server block, type the name of your news server. If you don't know what to put here, contact your system administrator.

2. In the News RC Directory field, enter a directory on your computer. The default is your Home Directory.

3. Click OK to save your changes.

**News RC**    Netscape and other Usenet newsreaders keep track of which newsgroups you read and which articles you've seen in the file *.newsrc*, usually in your Home Directory. Note the leading dot in the filename.

# ACCESSING NEWSGROUPS

Now that you've configured Netscape for newsgroups, click the Newsgroups Directory Button.

This takes you to the page showing you which newsgroups you are subscribed to. If you've read news in the past on your system, you probably already have a .newsrc file; the list of newsgroups you see is taken from that file. If you've never read news, the .newsrc file is created by Netscape, and you are automatically subscribed to three newsgroups.

Figure 16.2 shows the Subscribed Newsgroups page for users who haven't previously read news, with the standard three newsgroups listed. If you've been a news reader, the page reflects your .newsrc file, displaying your subscribed newsgroups.

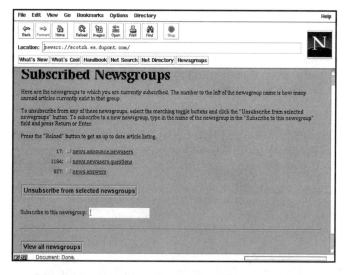

**FIGURE 16.2**    The Netscape Subscribed Newsgroups page.

**Subscribed**  When you subscribe to a newsgroup, it means you'll be able to read the articles in that newsgroup. Subscribed newsgroups appear on your Subscribed Newsgroups list. Since there are more than 10,000 newsgroups, you'll want to be selective in subscribing to avoid being overwhelmed.

There are a couple of things to notice about Figure 16.2:

- Each newsgroup shows a number, indicating the number of articles available in the newsgroup. As you read articles, these numbers decrease.

- There's a check box to the left of each newsgroup you can use to unsubscribe.

As stated above, there are thousands of newsgroups, but as a new reader, you only see three. How can you learn about the other groups? As you've surely guessed, click View all newsgroups for a screen like Figure 16.3.

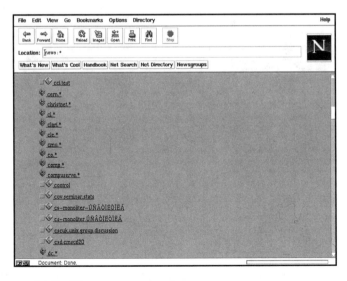

**FIGURE 16.3**  The newsgroups list.

You can see there are a couple of different icons displayed on this screen, as well as some check boxes. In addition, some of the listings are followed by an asterisk. Let's translate:

- The colored icons (and asterisks) signify a hierarchy of related newsgroups, such as comp.

- The other icons signify individual newsgroups.

Scroll down your listing to find the comp hierarchy and click it. This opens another listing of newsgroups and sub-divisions of the comp newsgroup tree. Find comp.infosystems. Select it, then select comp.infosystems.www. Finally, click comp.infosystems.www.browsers.x.

At last, you've reached a listing of news articles. It looks much like the one in Figure 16.4, although the article titles you'll see will be different.

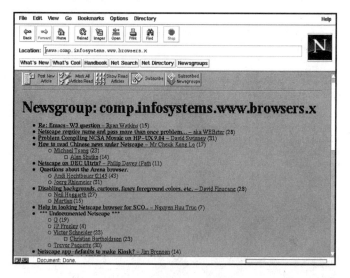

**FIGURE 16.4**   The comp.infosystems.www.browsers.x newsgroup.

You're no doubt eager to start reading some of these—as you can see, several of them deal with Netscape. Before you do, though, click Subscribe (on the upper right) for this important newsgroup. You'll pop back to the Subscribed Newsgroups page, where you'll notice comp.infosystems.www.browsers.x has been added to your list of subscribed groups.

**TIP** **Subscribing to Newsgroups Can Be a Tedious Process** You can make mass subscriptions by selecting check boxes of interesting newsgroups as you work your way down a newsgroup hierarchy, as you did in this lesson. Once you've selected a bunch on a given Newsgroups list, scroll down to the bottom and click Subscribe to selected newsgroups. This will add all you selected to your subscription list in a single step.

In this lesson you learned to configure Netscape for Usenet news. You also learned how to view the lists of newsgroups and subscribe to ones that look interesting. In the next lesson you will learn how to read and respond to news articles.

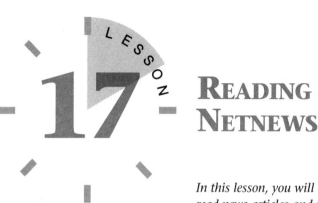

# LESSON 17 — READING NETNEWS

*In this lesson, you will learn how to read news articles and more about subscribing to newsgroups.*

## HOW NEWSGROUPS WORK

Reading, responding to, and posting Netnews with Netscape is easy, but you need an overview of how newsgroups work.

Usenet is divided into seven major categories:

- Computers
- Science
- Recreation
- Social Issues
- Talk
- News Itself
- Alternative Groups

Each is the tip of a vast iceberg of related newsgroups, subdivided into thousands of often-very-specialized topics. Besides the major groups—comp, sci, rec, soc, talk, news, and alt—you'll find biz (business), bionet (biology), misc (miscellaneous), and local groups.

Netnews users *post* articles to newsgroups. An article can be anything—a scholarly article, a recipe, or a diatribe about the best Web browser. News software places the article on the local system for others to read and also transmits it to other systems. Receiving systems pass the article along to other systems. Soon, often within a few hours, your news posting will reach thousands of other systems, where other users can read it.

# READING NEWS ITEMS

Let's continue where we left off in Lesson 16, with newsgroup comp.infosystems.www.browsers.x. This is a newsgroup about Web browser software, like Netscape, that runs on computers running X Windows, like your UNIX system. (There are newsgroups for Macintosh and PC/Windows browsers.) Take a look at Figure 17.1.

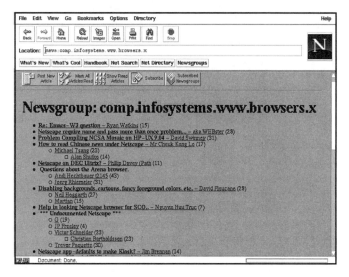

FIGURE 17.1    The comp.infosystems.www.browsers.x newsgroup.

Although Netscape's display of news articles is mostly plain text, notice that each listing is a hyperlink. Click one that looks interesting. Figure 17.2 is an example. It's a recurring article called a FAQ (Frequently Asked Questions) article about this newsgroup.

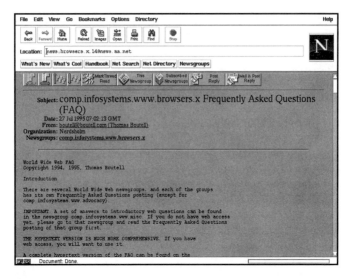

**FIGURE 17.2**    A Netnews article.

**Frequently Asked Questions**    More and more new users come into Usenet every day. The same questions crop up over and over. FAQs collect these common questions—and their answers—together. They're posted on a regular basis to newsgroups, so new users get the benefit of them and so old users don't have to see the same questions again and again.

Besides showing you how a news article looks (plain text), this one has substantive content; you'll want to look for it when you start reading Netnews. Notice there are several hyperlinks at the head of the article, including a link that allows you to send e-mail (see Lesson 20) to the poster. You'll also see a list of newsgroups to which the article was posted; some articles get posted to multiple groups.

What can you do with this article? Well, you can just read it, using the scroll bar to move down the screen. Your standard

Netscape tools for saving and printing pages work, so if you want to make a permanent copy of the article, you can.

How about if you'd like to respond to the article? Say you have a question that doesn't appear in the FAQ or you have a correction. Click the link with the author's name and e-mail address to send a private message to the poster. You can also post a follow-up article. Click the Post Reply button to do so. Figure 17.3 shows the initial screen you see when you do so.

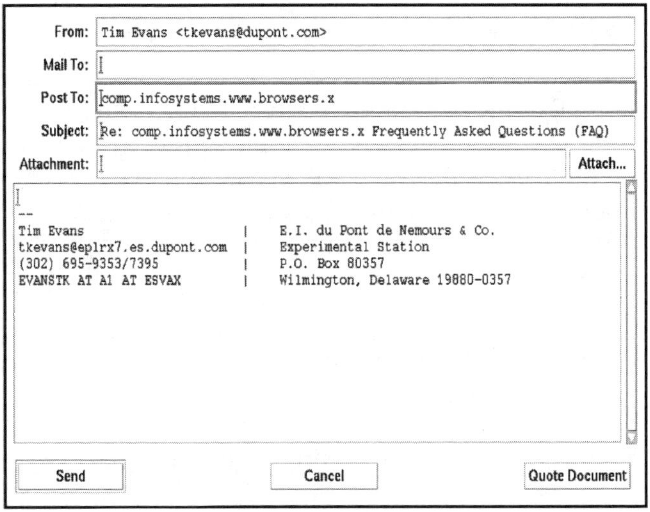

```
        From:  Tim Evans <tkevans@dupont.com>

      Mail To:  |

      Post To:  |comp.infosystems.www.browsers.x

      Subject:  |Re: comp.infosystems.www.browsers.x Frequently Asked Questions (FAQ)

   Attachment:  |                                                         Attach...

  |
  --
  Tim Evans                       |    E.I. du Pont de Nemours & Co.
  tkevans@eplrx7.es.dupont.com    |    Experimental Station
  (302) 695-9353/7395             |    P.O. Box 80357
  EVANSTK AT A1 AT ESVAX          |    Wilmington, Delaware 19880-0357



       Send              Cancel              Quote Document
```

**FIGURE 17.3**    Post a follow-up article.

As you can see, this is basically a text editor you use to make your follow-up posting. This editor is pretty crude. Among other things, it *appears* to do word wrap, like a word processor, but it really doesn't. As a result, your postings come out all on one long line if you don't press Return or Enter at the end of each line. You can use your mouse to highlight, delete, cut and paste, and so on, with this editor.

Notice some of the boxes in the editor screen are filled in for you, including the newsgroup name or original poster name. Use the

Quote Document button to include the original posting in your follow-up. Click Send when you've finished.

 **It Says "Mail"** Netscape uses the same editor for posting Netnews articles and sending e-mail; you'll see this again in Lesson 20.

# POSTING ORIGINAL ARTICLES

Besides follow-up postings, you can, of course, make original postings. Click This Newsgroup to return to the main article listing. Post New Article starts your posting, using the editor you saw in Figure 17.3, but with a slight difference. Your name and the newsgroup name are filled in, but there's no Subject. Use the editor to compose your article. Note the Attach... button, which allows you to attach an existing document. You can also post a news article by:

- Pulling down the File menu
- Selecting Mail Document
- Filling in the Post To: box with the newsgroup name
- Entering a Subject line and the text of your article

 **TIP** **Post-its** The row of buttons you see across the top of the screen appears at both the top and bottom of all news articles/article listings, so it's convenient when you've scrolled down a bit. Just use the position of the scroll bar to gauge how far from the top or bottom of the article you are.

## SUBSCRIBING/UNSUBSCRIBING TO NEWSGROUPS

In Lesson 16 you subscribed to the comp.infosystems.www. browsers.x newsgroup with the Subscribe button. Back up to the Newsgroup listing page, using either the Netscape's Back or This Newsgroup buttons. Notice what's happened to the Subscribe button. It now reads UnSubscribe. Any time you decide you don't want to look at a newsgroup any more, just unsubscribe.

**I Want a Newsgroup Back**   Remember from Lesson 16—you can browse through newsgroup hierarchies and read any article without having to be subscribed to a particular newsgroup. If you unsubscribe, you can resume your subscription. Similarly, you don't have to make all your subscription choices at once; you always have the ability to subscribe/unsubscribe. You always have access to the Subscribed Newsgroups listing.

## THREADS

If you're not already there, return to the article listing (click This Newsgroup). Most of the listings line up, right down the page. Some are indented, with several levels of indentation in places. As you've learned, anyone can post follow-up articles. Frequently, extended discussions—or threads—occur with multiple follow-ups, then subsequent follow-ups to the follow-ups. Netscape groups threads together and displays them using indentation. Some threads go on for months, possibly becoming flame wars, where people argue points strenuously, sometimes to the point of personal insult.

**Flame On**   Netnews postings in which users verbally abuse, or *flame*, others are considered poor Netiquette. You'll find periodic postings to the newsgroup **news. announce.newusers** outlining generally accepted Usenet courtesy and practice, including a tongue-in-cheek article called *Dear Emily Postnews*.

In the last two lessons, you've had a basic introduction to Netnews, using Netscape. Netscape is okay for occasional news browsing, but dedicated, full-feature newsreader programs are better. Ask your system administrator what others are installed. In the next lesson you will learn how to set up Netscape to view more graphical images.

# VIEWING AND SAVING GRAPHIC FILES

*In this lesson, you will learn how to work with graphical image files in Netscape.*

## USING NETSCAPE WITH GRAPHICS FILES

Netscape displays the most common kinds of graphical image files you will encounter on the Web. These include GIF (Graphical Exchange Format), JPEG (Joint Photographic Experts Graphics), and XBM (X Windows Bitmap) files. There are many other kinds of graphics files, however, because not all types of graphic formats are suitable for all applications. Vendors have developed their own graphical formats to suit their products.

### HELPER APPLICATIONS

Netscape doesn't handle all these kinds of graphical files, nor, of course, can it handle new ones developed in the future. Fortunately, the Netscape developers followed the lead of the designers of earlier Web browsers, adopting a standard way of dealing with unsupported data. Any Web browser, including Netscape, can be set up to hand unsupported data off to a Helper Application.

**Helper Applications**   Separate computer programs that take the data Web browsers can't interpret and deal with it, displaying unsupported images, or playing sound or video files.

There's a rich set of UNIX programs that can be set up as Netscape Helper applications. Some of them are standard operating system utilities, while others are freely available on the Internet for retrieval and installation. This book can only cover a few of them, but will mention a representative sample.

## SETTING UP A HELPER APPLICATION FOR VIEWING GRAPHICS FILES

We'll cover the steps of setting up Helper applications in the next few paragraphs. As we set up a graphical image viewer, you'll learn important information about Helper applications in general that'll be useful in later lessons.

John Cristy's package ImageMagick contains just such an image viewer, called display. Information about ImageMagick is available at this URL:

> **http://www.wizards.dupont.com/cristy/ ImageMagick.html**

Like most freely available UNIX software, this package is distributed in source code form, and must be compiled before you can run it on your system; it will build on virtually all UNIX systems. Ask your system administrator for help.

**Source Code and Compilation**   The original code for ImageMagick is written in the C Language that must be passed through a C compiler program to turn it from the original plain text source code into an executable machine language program that can be run on your system.

Here are the steps to setting up ImageMagick's *display* as a Netscape Helper application for viewing graphics files.

In Netscape pull down the Options menu, select Preferences, and then select Helper Applications. Figure 18.1 shows the Helper Applications dialog box.

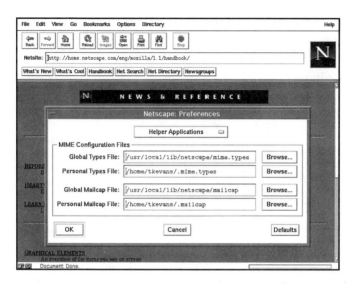

**FIGURE 18.1**   The Netscape Helper Applications dialog box.

UNIX Netscape does not have a graphical interface for setting up Helper applications. This dialog box doesn't do very much of anything, other than tell you there are two categories of something called MIME Configuration Files, the Types file, and the Mailcap file. Further, there are Global and Personal versions of each.

**MIME**   You may have run across MIME—Multi-Purpose Internet Mail Extensions—in the context of e-mail, where it's used to allow attachment of non-text files to e-mail messages for transmission over the Internet. SGI's Zmail is one MIME-compliant e-mail package for UNIX systems, as is the new Common Desktop Environment mailtool, now available on some UNIX systems, such as Sun's Solaris 2.5 and IBM's AIX 4.x.

The whole MIME/Helper application business is both tedious and important, especially since UNIX Netscape doesn't provide a graphical tool for setting up Helper applications. A little background can help. In Netscape, MIME is used for linking filename extensions to types of files and, from there, to Helper applications.

 **Extensions** Filename extensions are the part of a filename after the last period in the filename. You're accustomed to seeing filenames like **letter.txt** or **mydoc.html**. The matter to the right side of the period in these filenames is the extension.

Netscape already knows about a long list of standard filename extensions and associates each with a MIME file type. For example, the filename extension .xwd is associated with X Windows image files produced by the *xwd* (X Windows Dump) program. (See your system manual for information about *xwd*.) Here's the entry from the Global Types File for .xwd files:

    image/xwd      xwd

As you can see, this format of this file is simple, with *image* signifying an image file. The type of image is separated by a forward slash and the associated filename extension(s) are shown on the right. Look up the complete list of file types and associated filename extensions in the Global Types File.

Here's how to enable Netscape viewing of graphics files with *display* as a Helper application.

- First, check the Global Mailcap File, the name of which is shown in the Netscape Helper Applications dialog box, to see if *display* (or some other program) has already been set up as a Helper application for images. You can use the UNIX *more* or *pg* commands to view this file on your screen. Look for a line that begins with image/xwd; or image/*;. If you find it, there should be something to the right of the semicolon; if it says display %s, you're already set up to view graphics with *display*.

- If you didn't find *display* in the Global Mailcap File, or the
  file doesn't exist, set up *display* in your Personal Mailcap
  File. Usually called .mailcap (note the period in the
  filename), create this file with any text editor, such as *vi*,
  *emacs*, or Sun's *textedit* editor. Add the following line,
  making sure to include the semicolon:

    **image/*; display %s**

**Global Files Help Everyone**    As you might guess, the
Global Mailcap File sets Helper applications for all users
on a UNIX system. Your system administrator can set up
common Helper applications and make them available
to everyone on the system. This minimizes the need for
users to set up and maintain Personal Mailcap Files. If
both files exist, your Personal Mailcap File overrides any
conflicts with the Global File.

Note the use of the asterisk here as a wild card, meaning that you
want to use *display* as your Helper application for all images in
Netscape.

Figure 18.2 shows use of *display* as a Helper application. As you
can see, two identical Netscape displays are tiled, one on top of
the other. The bottom image is an original Netscape display. After
the page was loaded, *xwd* was used to capture the window in a
local file. Netscape was asked to open the image file (File, Open
File). Using *display* as its Helper application, Netscape opens a
second window (note the *ImageMagick* legend in the title bar)
with the image displayed.

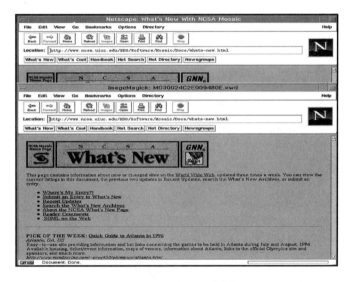

FIGURE 18.2    Netscape with display as Helper application.

## SETTING UP A HELPER APPLICATION FOR POSTSCRIPT FILES

PostScript is a widely used graphic format. Defined as a device-independent standard for representing the printed page, you may think of PostScript in the context of printers. It's useful, however, to view PostScript documents on-screen, and many documents on the World Wide Web are in PostScript. So, having a PostScript viewer as a Netscape Helper application is important.

Some UNIX systems include PostScript viewers as a standard part of the operating system. These include Sun's Solaris 2.x imagetool, SunOS 4.1.x pageview, and IBM's showps. You may also have the freeware package ghostscript installed on your system, although it's not a standard part of any vendor's operating system.

To enable *imagetool* as a Netscape Helper application for viewing PostScript files, add the following entry to either the Global or your Personal Mailcap File:

**application/postscript;imagetool %s**

The standard MIME types file contains a mapping of the PostScript file type to the filename extensions .ps, .eps, and .ai.

In this lesson, you learned how to configure Netscape to use Helper applications to view graphic files, including PostScript files. In the next lesson you will learn about Netscape security, including how to use Netscape to go shopping on the Internet.

# 19

# SECURITY AND SHOPPING WITH NETSCAPE

*In this lesson, you will learn about Netscape's security features and how they can help you do business or go shopping on the World Wide Web.*

Netscape has important security features. These features allow you to conduct confidential transactions over the Internet:

- Companies transmitting confidential business information between sites or with customers

- Financial institutions making funds transfers

- Ordinary people shopping on the Web with their credit cards

## WHY IS SECURITY IMPORTANT?

The Internet is a vast, global network, with hundreds of thousands, if not millions, of points of entry. Almost anyone can connect. Your data flowing across the Internet takes a wide variety of paths between you and its destination, including flowing across public network gateways where snoopers can scan the data with sophisticated equipment. Worse, with few exceptions, the data flowing across the Internet is in plain text, readable by anyone with the right equipment.

**Snoopers and Sniffers**  Hardware or software installed, legally or illegally, that can collect user passwords, credit card numbers, and other sensitive information as it crosses the Internet. Your network may have a sniffer running somewhere and even your network administrators may not know it.

In this context, businesses and consumers alike are loath to conduct confidential transactions across the Internet. A bank would hesitate to make million-dollar electronic fund transfers over an insecure network, with the transfer both unverifiable and subject to redirection. So you should hesitate to give your MasterCard or VISA number to a stranger who calls on the phone—or who asks you to type it into a fill-in form on the Web.

## Netscape Security

How does Netscape provide security in this environment?

- Netscape can authenticate Web servers, allowing you to be sure you are really communicating with the Bank of America, Land's End, or The Sharper Image.

- When communicating with an authenticated server, Netscape encrypts the information flow; only your computer and the server can make sense of it.

 **Help!**  Netscape Help has detailed security information.

If you've purchased Netscape directly from Netscape Communications and are in the United States, the version you received has substantially improved RSA Encryption (the downloaded version has a crippled RSA encryption). Figure 19.1 shows the non-export version of Netscape's startup screen, with the RSA Encryption notice.

 **RSA Encryption**  Rivest-Shamir-Adleman Encryption is based on two special "keys." One is public—you give yours out to everyone—while the other is private for each person. It takes both keys to decrypt a message that's been RSA-encrypted. If Joe sends you an encrypted message, you use Joe's public key and *your* private key to decrypt it. Because of U.S. export regulations (RSA Encryption is considered a military weapon), only a limited version of it is available in the version of Netscape you can download on the Internet. Full-blown RSA Encryption is available only when you purchase Netscape, and you must do so in the United States.

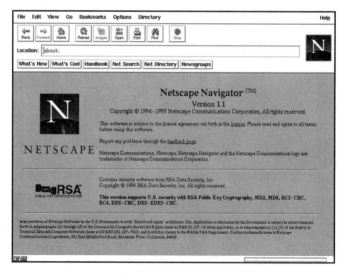

**Figure 19.1**  The Netscape Security page.

Even though you have a version of Netscape that supports secure transactions, you still need to make sure the Web server with which you're communicating can be authenticated. Figure 19.2 is an enlargement of the lower left-hand corner of Figure 19.1. Note the broken-key icon, which signifies that the page is from an unauthenticated Web server. If the server is authenticated, the key would be unbroken.

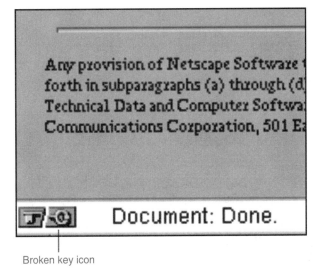

Broken key icon

FIGURE 19.2    The Netscape page detail showing the broken key icon.

You can further verify the security of any given Web document within Netscape from the File, Document Information command. Figure 19.3 shows a typical display; note the Security Information (in this case, the message "This is an insecure document").

Netscape gives you yet another means of ensuring security. When you type information, such as your American Express card number, into a Web fill-in form and go to submit it, Netscape will warn you if the Web server involved isn't secure. Figure 19.4 shows this warning.

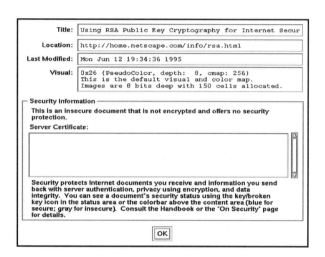

FIGURE **19**.3    Netscape document information.

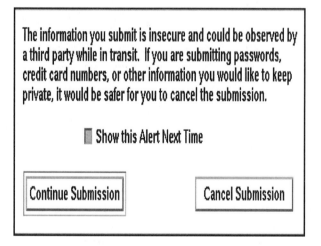

FIGURE **19**.4    Netscape security warning on a fill-in form.

**Netscape Security Broken?**  As this manuscript went to production, there was a report of Netscape's exportable RSA encryption having been broken. Cryptographer Hal Finney of the California Institute of Technology, independently of Netscape Communications Corporation, had announced a Challenge. The encrypted message he created was broken using parallel decryption techniques on more than 100 UNIX systems. Most UNIX users don't have access to this brute-force computing power, but people in mid-size and larger companies, academic institutions, and other organizations do. As of the time this manuscript went to production, none of Netscape's Web FAQs or other public pages have addressed the question of encryption having been broken with relative ease. Read more about this at this URL:

http://www.portal.com/~hfinney/sslchal.html

# WHICH WEB SERVERS ARE SECURE?

At present, even secure Netscape cannot guarantee the security of any Web server other than the one sold by Netscape Communications Corp., which implements Netscape's own security mechanisms. Netscape will not help you communicate securely with other Web servers. This catch-22, however, is being remedied. A number of Web vendors, including Netscape, have worked out a set of standards for secure Web transactions, and you can look for other vendors' secure servers soon.

The two largest U.S. credit card companies—MasterCard and VISA —have also entered into an agreement for ensuring secure use of card numbers on the Web. This is a fast-moving area with money to be made, so expect new developments soon.

## SHOPPING AND SELLING ON THE WORLD WIDE WEB

Thus forewarned, you can go shopping safely—or make your products available to shoppers—on the Web. Because you're running UNIX Netscape, you might be interested in the wide range of UNIX and X Windows reference books available from Macmillan Publishing via their online catalog at **http://www.mcp.com/ cgi-bin/do-bookstore.cgi**. See Figure 19.5.

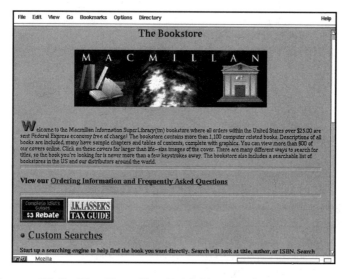

**FIGURE 19.5**    The Macmillan Publishing catalog.

If you follow the links here, you'll see you can order books online from Macmillan only by pre-establishing an account. Once you've done so, there is a fill-in form for ordering. This is a common practice for shopping outlets on the Web to ensure security of credit card numbers. When secure Web servers and clients become more widely available, this extra step should disappear.

# LOCATING ONLINE SHOPPING OUTLETS

One of the best ways to locate shopping opportunities—or to check out your competition—on the Web is the Yahoo database (see Lesson 10). A Yahoo keyword search on "shopping" turned up more than 220 hits. See Figure 19.6.

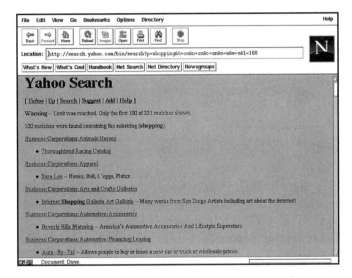

FIGURE 19.6    A Yahoo keyword search on "shopping."

For an overall Web shopping guide with links to lots of companies doing business on the Web, see **http:// www.shopping2000.com/**. Here, you'll find online catalogs organized into major categories. Figure 19.7 shows the Shopping2000 startup page.

You can see the potential for businesses to sell on the Web, and the corresponding opportunities for shopping, even though adequate security arrangements are not yet widely in place.

**FIGURE 19.7** The Shopping2000 home page.

In this lesson, you learned how Netscape implements security for online shopping and other business transactions on the Web. In the next lesson you will learn how to use Netscape to send electronic mail on the Internet.

# Sending Electronic Mail Using Netscape

*In this lesson, you will learn how to use Netscape to send e-mail to other Internet users.*

E-mail is one of the oldest—and still one of the most heavily used—Internet services. It's one of the primary reasons people go online.

## How Does E-Mail Work?

UNIX systems have e-mail built in. In the early days, users on the same system sent messages to each other. Soon, people wanted to send e-mail to users on remote systems, so programs for delivering e-mail over phone lines and modems were built. When the Internet developed, systems were adapted to deliver e-mail over the Net.

Many UNIX programs allow users to send and read e-mail. These range from very simple text-based programs to fancy graphical ones. Figure 20.1 shows the Common Desktop Environment's mailtool, coming soon to a UNIX system near you.

## Configuring Netscape to Send E-Mail

While your UNIX system probably has several full-featured e-mail packages installed, you can use Netscape to send e-mail. Netscape's mail feature is somewhat limited, but it can be handy. You need to do a little setup first, though, using Netscape

Preferences, Select Mail and News. Your screen should look like
Figure 20.2.

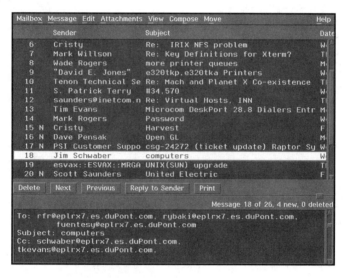

**FIGURE 20.1**    A graphical e-mail tool.

**FIGURE 20.2**    The Mail and News preferences dialog box.

As you can see, there are several blanks for you to fill in; some may already be filled in by the system. Let's work our way through these. You may need to get some of the required information from your system administrator.

> Mail (SMTP) Server   You probably don't need to enter anything. UNIX systems have the ability to deliver e-mail built in. Your system administrator may want you to route your outgoing e-mail through a central mail server. If so, type it in here.

> Your Name   This field may already be filled in, but if it's not, type your name as you want it to appear (e.g., Joseph H. Brown, III).

> Your E-mail   Type your e-mail address. It should be in the form *userid@systemname*, where userid is your login ID on the system, and *systemname* is the name of your local system or central mail server.

> Organization   This is an optional field; type in your organization name if you want.

> Signature File   Also optional, this is the name of a file containing your e-mail *signature*.

> Send and Post   Accept the default setting of *Allow 8-bit*. (See the last tip in this lesson for an exception to this.)

Click OK to close the Mail and News preferences dialog box.

**Signature Files**   *Signatures* are an e-mail tradition. These contain some *brief* information about you. Some use them to include phone and fax numbers and/or postal addresses. Others include a quotation or a personal expression. Be sure to keep your signature file short; four lines of text is a good rule of thumb. Also, remember your signature file is *automatically attached to all messages*. A Pearl Jam or Barbara Streisand song lyric may express your feelings, but do your boss and business associates really need to see it on every message?

# SENDING E-MAIL

You're now ready to send e-mail with Netscape. Pull down the File menu and select Mail Document to open the Send Mail/Post News dialog box, as shown in Figure 20.3.

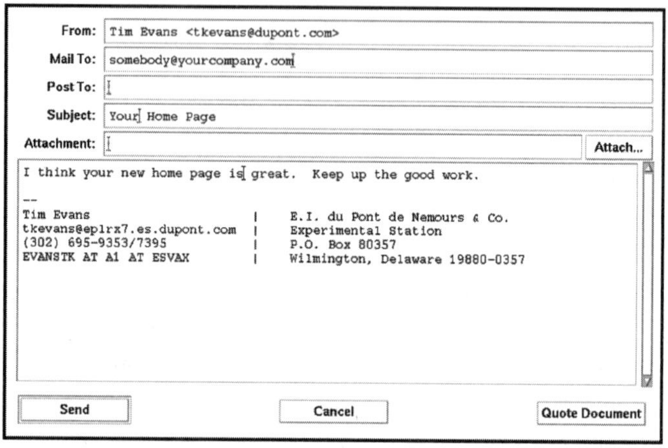

| From: | Tim Evans <tkevans@dupont.com> |
| Mail To: | somebody@yourcompany.com |
| Post To: | |
| Subject: | Your Home Page |
| Attachment: | |

```
I think your new home page is great.  Keep up the good work.

--
Tim Evans                       |   E.I. du Pont de Nemours & Co.
tkevans@eplrx7.es.dupont.com    |   Experimental Station
(302) 695-9353/7395             |   P.O. Box 80357
EVANSTK AT A1 AT ESVAX          |   Wilmington, Delaware 19880-0357
```

Send          Cancel          Quote Document

**FIGURE 20.3**   Netscape mail.

As you can see, this box comes up partially filled in, with the information from your Preferences. Your name and e-mail address are in the From box and your signature file is entered into the text box. The Subject line may also be filled in.

Fill in the e-mail address of your addressee, in the form *user@system.domain*, in Mail To. For example, to send e-mail to Netscape (the address is at the bottom of the Netscape home page) use **info@netscape.com**.

Although Subject is an optional field, it's a good idea to use it to give the recipient an idea of what your e-mail is about.

Since one major purpose of Netscape's e-mail feature is to let you send a copy of a Web page to someone, you'll see Subject comes up filled in with the title of the page you're viewing. To send the page, click Quote Document to read it in.

**What Are Those Funny Characters?**  You'll notice each line of the text is preceded by a greater than (>) sign, as in Figure 20.4. This is yet another Internet e-mail tradition, identifying quoted material in a message. Add any comments to the message, without the character, and you can see how the different parts of the message stand out.

| From: | Tim Evans <tkevans@dupont.com> | |
|---|---|---|
| Mail To: | myfriend@yourcompany.com | |
| Post To: | | |
| Subject: | DuPont Home Page | |
| Attachment: | | Attach... |

```
> [Image]
>
> What's New    Technology    UNIX Support    Other DW2 Servers
> Download Client and Server Software    Access WWW    Miscellaneous
>
> Welcome to DuPont-Wide Web!
>
> Welcome to DuPont-Wide Web (DW2). DW2 is a searchable "living document,"
> accessible via the DuPont corporate network. Created by Central Science &
> Engineering, DW2 allows "multimedia" information (text, images, graphics,
> animations, and sounds) to be easily and instantly accessed by anyone within
> the Company. Click with your mouse on any highlighted/underscored word or
> phrase to follow the hyperlink.
>
> [Image]
```

| Send | Cancel | Quote Document |
|---|---|---|

**FIGURE 20.4**   Quote Document.

Change the Subject line, if necessary, and then type in your message or any comments to go with the included text. You can use your mouse to edit either.

Besides including a file in your message with Quote Document, Netscape allows you to attach files to e-mail messages.

**Quote Document, Attach File?** There's a small, but significant, difference. *Quote Document* means to read the document into the text box, where you can see and edit it. *Attach* means to send the file along with your message, but doesn't bring it up into the text box and, hence, doesn't let you edit it.

The Attach Document dialog box is shown in Figure 20.5. You have several choices here. First, the choice of Document or File. The former refers to Web documents, and gives you the option of sending the document in one of three formats—plain text, HTML document source (i.e., with Hypertext Markup Language codes), and PostScript. If you choose PostScript, the document will be printable with all the graphical features you see when viewing it with Netscape, provided your addressee has a PostScript printer.

Add the following attachment after the message:

⊙ Document: http://dw2.es.dupont.com/

Attach As:
○ Document Text
⊙ Document Source
○ PostScript

○ File: [ ]    Browse...

Attach    Cancel

**FIGURE 20.5**    The Attach Document dialog box.

The second major choice in the Attach Document dialog box is File. This allows you to attach any file on your local system. Click the File button, and then fill in the full pathname of the file to be attached. If you're not sure of the location of the file, use Browse to rummage around until you find the file you want.

**Plain Text and Binary Files**   You can attach any file, even non-text files, such as executable program files or files from an application such as a word processor. Before you send a binary file, be sure your recipient can deal with it. Netscape does a special conversion on binary files to allow them to pass as e-mail. Your recipient needs to be able to reverse this conversion. If you have problems, try going back to the Netscape Mail Preferences and selecting MIME Compliant (Quoted Printable).

Once you're done creating your e-mail message, click Send to ship it off to its destination.

# ONE-WAY E-MAIL

There is one problem with Netscape e-mail. You can send e-mail, but you can't read it. To read your e-mail, use one of your system's built-in mail readers. Full-featured mailers are more useful than Netscape's limited mail feature.

In this lesson, you learned how to use Netscape to send e-mail messages. In the next lesson you will learn how to add multimedia sound capabilities to Netscape.

# CONFIGURING NETSCAPE TO PLAY WEB PAGE AUDIO

*In this lesson, you will learn how to configure Netscape to play audio (sound) files you find on the Web.*

## AUDIO ON THE WORLD-WIDE WEB

You'll often find Web pages with links to audio files. Examples include voice messages like the one from U.S. President Clinton on the White House home page (see Lesson 2). Other Web sites have musical recordings. Because the Web is a multimedia system, you'll want to know how to set up Netscape to deal with these sound files.

### GETTING SOUND OUT OF YOUR UNIX WORKSTATION

Before you can get sound out of the Web, your UNIX workstation must have a loudspeaker. Some systems have minimal speakers, good only for beeps; these won't do for the audio files with which you're concerned here. Many late-model UNIX workstations are equipped with good-quality speakers. Some speakers are built in, while others are external. If you're running Linux or another PC UNIX, you'll need a sound card supported by your version of UNIX and speakers. The range of possibilities is too large to cover here, so I'll assume you have an adequate speaker on your system.

## UNIX AUDIO PLAYER PROGRAMS

Also, you need to make sure you have an audio-playing program on your system and that it's set up as a Netscape Helper application. Some UNIX vendors include a basic sound-playing program with their operating system. Sun, for example, provides audiotool and SGI provides sfplay, while HP-UX includes acontrol. (The latter is undocumented in HP-UX 9.x, and is squirreled away in the directory **/usr/audio**, so you'll have to dig it out.) These programs work like a tape recorder, displaying on-screen start/ stop buttons.

A no-cost audio player that works on most UNIX systems is AudioFile, which is available at the URL **ftp://gatekeeper. dec.com/pub/DEC/AF**. Although AudioFile was developed by people at Digital Equipment Corporation, it supports different UNIX systems.

## CONFIGURING NETSCAPE FOR SOUND

Just as in Lesson 18, when you configured Netscape to use a Helper application to display graphics files, you need to configure Netscape to use a Helper application to play sound files. Figure 21.1 shows the Helper Applications preferences dialog box.

As you learned in Lesson 18, there's no point-and-click tool for setting up Helper applications in UNIX Netscape. The Browse buttons don't do much of anything here. Instead, you or your System Administrator need to hand-edit either the Global or Personal Types and Mailcap files. Use your favorite text editor. Here are the steps; we'll use Sun's audiotool in this example. (You can substitute your system's audio player program—SGI's sfplay, for example—for audiotool.)

Check the Global and Personal Types files for an audio entry. It should look something like this:

**audio/basic      au snd**

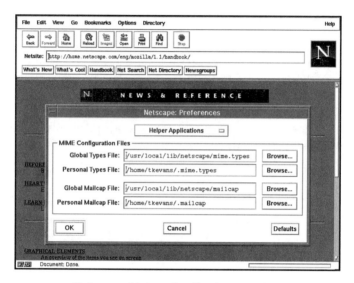

**FIGURE 21.1**    Netscape Helper Applications preferences.

As you'll recall, the Types file maps MIME types with filename extensions. The MIME type audio/basic is mapped to the filename extensions .au or .snd. Add the entry to the Types file, if necessary.

Next, check the Global and Personal Mailcap files for an audio entry. It should look like this:

**audio/basic;    /usr/openwin/bin/audiotool**

The Mailcap file takes the MIME-type and filename extension information in the Types file and associates it with a computer program. Thus, in this example, you're associating filenames ending in .au or .snd with the audio MIME type, and telling Netscape to use audiotool to play them. Add the entry to the Mailcap file, if necessary (don't miss that semicolon).

**Global Versus Personal Types and Mailcap Files**

TIP    Your system administrator can save a great deal of everyone's time by setting up the Global Types and Mailcap files to include common MIME types and Helper applications. Global files apply to everyone on the system; don't duplicate them for your Personal files. Use your Personal files only to override the Global files when you need to. Personal files always take precedence when there is a conflict with the Global ones.

# TRYING OUT YOUR AUDIO HELPER APPLICATION

Now that you've set up an audio Helper application, you'll want to try it out. Before you do, open the Netscape preferences dialog box and click the OK button. This tells Netscape to re-read the Global and Personal Types and Mailcap files, which you've just changed.

Next, try out the following URL:

**http://www.paramount.com/VoyagerIntro.html**

This is Paramount Pictures' Star Trek Voyager home page, and it's shown in Figure 21.2.

Scroll down the page to where it says "A Message from Kate Mulgrew!" and click either of the two links, au 8kHz 49k or 11kHz 68k. (See Figure 21.3.)

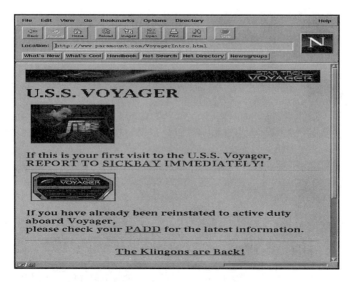

**FIGURE 21.2**    The Star Trek Voyager home page.

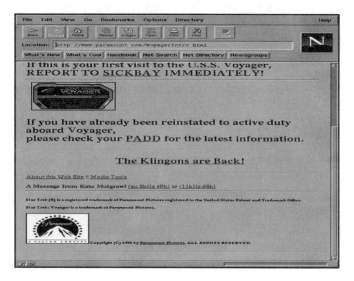

**FIGURE 21.3**    Hyperlinks to sound files.

Within a few seconds, the sound file downloads and audiotool pops up on your screen, as shown in Figure 21.4. Click the Start button to play the message from Kate Mulgrew.

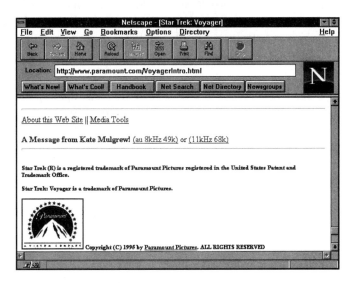

**FIGURE 21.4**   Sun's audiotool.

**No Viewer Configured for File Type: audio/basic. Did not hear sound!**   This error message indicates that you missed a step or incorrectly configured the Helper application. Go back and review the instructions, and then try again. If things still don't work, double-check the connectors and volume control on your speaker.

# DIFFERENT KINDS OF AUDIO FILES

So far, the discussion of audio has dealt only with the basic audio file format defined by Sun Microsystems and supported on other UNIX systems. You'll find, however, other kinds of audio files on the Web. One of the most common is the PC .wav format. Sun's audiotool doesn't support this audio format. To support this and other audio formats, you'll need to install another audio Helper application, such as AudioFile, which was mentioned previously. Alternatively, ask your system administrator for help in setting up a custom Netscape Helper application that uses an audio file conversion utility. SGI's sfconvert and Sun's audioconvert are two examples.

In this lesson, you learned how to configure Netscape to play sound files. In the next lesson you will learn how to configure Netscape full-motion video.

# Configuring Netscape to Play Full-Motion Video

LESSON

*22*

*In this lesson, you will learn how to configure Netscape to play full-motion video you find on the Web.*

The vast majority of the pictures you'll currently find on the Web are static images. You will find, however, many full-motion video files on the Web. Like audio, Netscape can't handle video directly, but it's easy to set up Helper applications so you can view the videos you find.

## Configuring Netscape for Full-Motion Video

Fortunately, your system does not need any special equipment to display the full-motion video files you will encounter on the Web. (Full-motion video with sound will, of course, require sound capabilities, as described in Lesson 21.) You've probably already correctly guessed that Netscape needs a Helper application to display full-motion video files. The most widely used MPEG viewer for UNIX is called mpeg_play, (yes, that is an underscore character in the name) and is available at the following URL:

**ftp://tr-ftp.cs.berkeley.edu/pub/multimedia/mpeg**

You'll find documentation on how to compile and install mpeg_play, as well as the source code, in the file **bmt1r1.tar.gz**. (The exact name may change if newer releases become available.)

**gz?**    The file **bmt1r1.tar.gz** has been compressed with a relatively new compression utility called *gzip*. You may need to retrieve the gzip source code and install it on your system so you can use gzip's companion—gunzip. Check with your system administrator. gzip is available at no cost at the URL **ftp://prep.ai.mit.edu/pub/gnu**.

After you've installed mpeg_play in a directory that's accessible to you, you're ready to configure it as a Netscape Helper application. Refer to Lessons 18 and 20 for detailed instructions about the Global and Personal Types and Mailcap files, which set up Helper applications on UNIX systems. The procedure here is much the same.

First, check the Global Types file for a **video** entry. It should look like this:

> **video/mpeg    mpeg mpg mpe**

**There's No video/mpeg Entry, but There Is a video/\* Entry**    The asterisk is a *wild card* here, indicating the entry applies to any kind of video. While you may find such a wild card entry specifying mpeg_play or another program, use the specific entry for video/mpeg for the time being.

As you'll recall, the Types file associates filename extensions with types of data files. In this case, the extensions .mpeg, .mpg, and .mpe are linked to MPEG video files. If there's no entry, your system administrator can add one to the Global Types file so everyone can access it, or you can add one to your Personal Types file.

Next, look for an MPEG viewer set up in the Global Mailcap file. It should look like this:

> **video/mpeg;    mpeg_play %s**

The Mailcap file links computer programs to the data type/
filename extension pairs from the Types file. Together, this de-
fines your Helper applications. Again, if there's no entry, your
system administrator can add one to the Global Mailcap file so
everyone can access it, or you can add one to your Personal
Mailcap file.

# VIEWING MPEG FULL-MOTION VIDEO

Now, to test your newly installed Helper application, jump to a
Web site that has MPEG full-motion video files. Try this URL:

> **http://clunix.cl.msu.edu/weather/**

This is a specialized Web server at Michigan State University that
provides weather information, including forecasts, satellite and
radar images like you see on TV, weather broadcasts, and, most
important, full-motion MPEG video files. Figure 22.1 shows this
page.

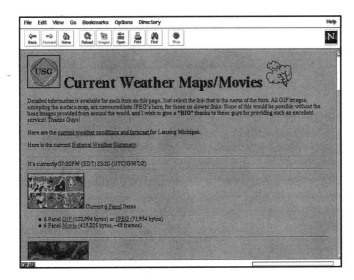

FIGURE 22.1   Current Weather Maps/Movies.

There are several MPEG movies on this page; scroll down to any link labeled Movie and click it. When the file is downloaded, Netscape will launch mpeg_play, as you see in Figure 22.2.

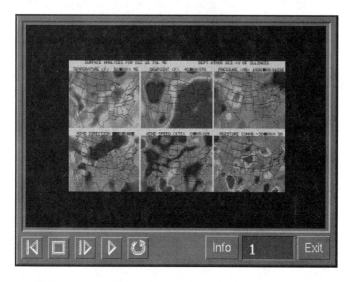

**FIGURE 22.2** mpeg_play.

 **It's Taking a Long Time to Download This File!** MPEG files (and full-motion video files in general, for that matter) tend to be quite large. It may take several minutes to download even small video files, even on high-speed Internet links.

As you can see, mpeg_play looks a lot like your home VCR—it has play, stop, and rewind buttons. Just click the start button to play the video.

# OTHER KINDS OF VIDEO

If you've ever used a Macintosh, you probably know about QuickTime videos. *QuickTime* is widely used on Macintoshes for full-motion video. It is one of several other kinds of video files you'll find on the Web. mpeg_play can't handle QuickTime or other video types. A good all-purpose video player for UNIX systems that handles QuickTime is Mark Podlipec's xanim, which is available at this URL:

> **http://www.portal.com/~podlipec/**
> **xa_features.html**

You can set up xanim as your video Helper application in the same way you do with mpeg_play. Because it can play several kinds of video, you may want to use xanim for all video, including MPEG video, and not use mpeg_play at all. To do this, check the Global Mailcap file for a wild card video entry, like this:

> **video/*;  xanim %s**

The asterisk indicates that you want xanim to be used to display all video. Refer back to your Global Types file for a list of video types and filename extensions. It probably looks something like this (there may be several other entries):

> **video/mpeg**            **mpeg mpg mpe**
>
> **video/quicktime**       **qt mov**

If you don't see a wild card entry for video in the Global Mailcap file, ask your system administrator to add one so all users on the system can access it, or add one to your Personal Mailcap file.

In this lesson, you learned how to configure a Netscape Helper application to play full-motion video. In the next lesson, you will learn how to change the appearance of Netscape to suit your own preferences.

# MAKING NETSCAPE LOOK LIKE YOU WANT IT TO

*In this lesson, you will learn how to personalize the appearance of Netscape.*

There are a number of ways you can personalize the look of Netscape on your screen. These range from the size and position of the Netscape window to the font styles and sizes that Netscape uses. In addition, you can control Netscape's background color and maximize the amount of information it can display.

## DISPLAYING MORE IN YOUR NETSCAPE SCREEN

Netscape uses a lot of on-screen real estate to display its various bells and whistles, in particular, the Toolbar, Directory Buttons, and Location field. All these features of Netscape are convenient when you're just starting out. After a while, you might want to suppress the routine display of one or more of these items, especially since all these functions are easily available from Netscape's pull-down menus. When you do, you gain a lot more space in the Netscape window for actual Web documents.

### REMOVING THE TOOLBAR

The nine icons that make up Netscape's Toolbar (Back, Forward, Home, and so on) are shortcuts to commands that appear on the File, Edit, View, and Go menus. Suppressing display of the

Toolbar allows you to see more of the current page. To remove
the Toolbar:

1. Select the Options menu.

2. Click Show Toolbar to remove the Toolbar.

The Toolbar disappears right away. Once you've made this
change, pull down the Options menu once again and note how
the appearance of the little box on the Show Toolbar line has
changed, showing you that the Toolbar feature has been
turned off.

## REMOVING THE LOCATION FIELD

The Location field displays the URL, or Uniform Resource Locator,
of the current page. While this information is helpful, it's not
essential, and neither is its on-screen display. If you suppress it,
you can see even more of your screen. Follow these steps:

1. Select the Options menu.

2. Click Show Location to remove the Location field.

## REMOVING THE DIRECTORY BUTTONS

The Directory Buttons (What's New, What's Cool, and so on)
duplicate commands available to you on the Directory and Help
menus. Removing this row of buttons will allow you to see still
more of your screen. Follow these steps:

1. Select the Options menu.

2. Click Show Directory Buttons to remove the Directory
   Buttons.

With the Toolbar, Location field, and Directory Buttons removed,
you can now view about one-third more of the current page. How
much more depends on the size of your Netscape window; it can
be as much as half. Figures 23.1 and 23.2 show the changes before
and after. You can, of course, suppress only one or two of these
three items—whichever suits you.

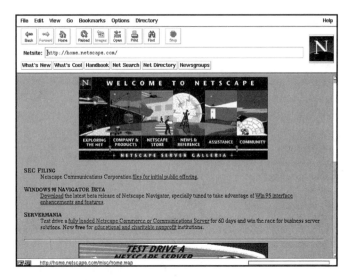

**FIGURE 23.1**    Netscape with the Toolbar, Location field, and Directory Buttons.

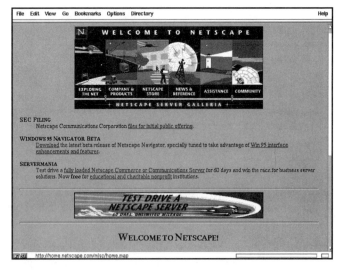

**FIGURE 23.2**    Netscape without the Toolbar, Location field, and Directory Buttons.

## MAKING TOOLBAR, LOCATION FIELD, AND DIRECTORY BUTTONS CHANGES PERMANENT

So far, the changes you've made to suppress display of the Toolbar, Location field, and/or Directory Buttons are *temporary*. When you exit Netscape, these changes will disappear unless you save them. Pull down the Options menu, and then select Save Options. This will save your Toolbar, Location field, and Directory Buttons setup for future Netscape sessions. As you'd expect, you can turn any of the features back on later, either temporarily or permanently.

# CHANGING FONTS, WINDOW SIZE, AND COLORS

UNIX Netscape provides some preferences for selecting font sizes used to display text. In addition, there are a couple of other simple ways of setting fonts and/or colors, along with some more complex ones.

### FONT SELECTION

Netscape's Windows and Link Styles Preferences dialog box allows you a choice of several font sizes. In Figure 23.3, you'll notice a set of Font Style click-buttons, labeled Small through Huge. Most of the figures in this book (see Figure 23.2, for example) use the Large font. Figure 23.4 shows the Medium font size selected.

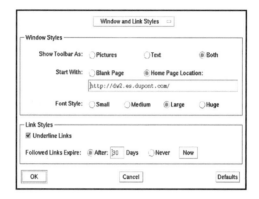

**FIGURE 23.3**    The Windows and Link Style Preferences dialog box.

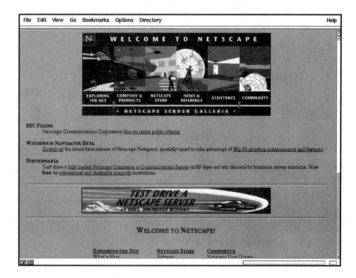

**FIGURE 23.4**    Netscape's Medium font size.

## WINDOW SIZE

You can change the size of your running Netscape window by dragging a corner of the window, the same as you do with any other X Windows program. To start Netscape with a particular window size, use a *command-line option*. If your workstation has a large, high-resolution monitor, you might start Netscape in a large, 1024-by-768-pixels window, like this:

    netscape -geometry 1024x768 &

**Command-Line Options**   Like most UNIX programs, you can control the behavior of Netscape by giving it options on the command line when you start it. Experienced X Windows users may want to add a startup line for Netscape, with your preferred command-line options, to your X Windows startup file, so it starts up every time you start X Windows. You'll find a list of the options Netscape knows about in the Frequently Asked Questions document, which is available on the Netscape Help pull-down menu.

## COLORS

UNIX Netscape has only one easy way of letting you change on-screen colors. You can select the background color with another command-line option at startup time. The figures in this book were made with Netscape using a white background to enhance their appearance. Here's how to start Netscape with a white background:

    netscape -bg white &

## NETSCAPE X RESOURCES

Besides command-line options, Netscape supports a large number of X Windows Resources, with which you can control many aspects of Netscape's operation and on-screen appearance. The subject of X Resources is too complex for this book, so you'll want to check your local system manuals or an X reference book, such as Sams Publishing's *UNIX Unleashed*. Briefly, Netscape resources are listed in a file installed on your system with Netscape. A common location for this file is the **/usr/lib/X11/app-defaults** directory; Sun, however, puts it in **/usr/openwin/lib/X11/ app-defaults**. The file is named **Netscape**. You'll find a lot of documentation in this file in the form of comments.

**System-Wide Resources** Installing Netscape X Resources allows you to make permanent changes (such as background color, screen size, and many others), saving you from having to enter command-line options every time you start the program. Your system administrator can implement common Netscape resources system-wide.

In this lesson, you learned how to make changes in Netscape's screen appearance. The next lesson continues with several other Netscape configuration subjects.

# ADVANCED NETSCAPE CONFIGURATION

*In this lesson, you will learn how to make more advanced configuration changes in Netscape.*

Having learned the basics of Netscape, including the customizations you've learned in the last few lessons, you may never need to tinker with Netscape. On the other hand, you may want to continue to tailor Netscape.

## USING NETSCAPE IN A SECURED NETWORK

As you learned in Lesson 19, Internet security is a major problem. Your network administrators may have installed a *firewall* system. If so, you'll need to set up Netscape to deal with this. Otherwise, you won't be able to access Web servers outside your local network.

**Firewall** As the name implies, an Internet firewall is a protective mechanism sitting between your LAN and the Internet. Firewalls protect networks by allowing only specified network traffic between the internal network and the Internet. Most firewall systems are set up to allow e-mail and some outgoing services, such as World Wide Web services, but in a controlled way.

Web services are safely passed through firewalls using a *proxy* system. Here's how this works:

- A proxy is a Web server running inside your LAN.

- The firewall allows *only* the proxy to communicate with the outside world.

- Netscape addresses requests to the proxy.

- The proxy contacts outside Web servers and relays the results to Netscape.

This sounds complicated, but is easy to set up in Netscape. Select the Options menu, click Preferences, and then click Proxies. Figure 24.1 shows the Proxies dialog box. If your system administrator is on the ball, you'll find the boxes in this form already filled in with proxy information for your network. Otherwise, you'll need to fill in the appropriate information.

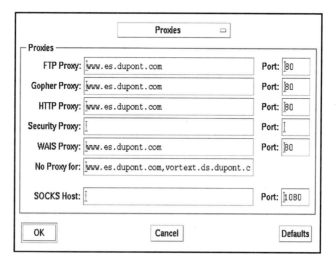

**FIGURE 24.1**    The Netscape Proxies dialog box.

Fill in the blanks (don't forget the Port boxes). Don't use the proxy host shown in Figure 24.1; it's appropriate for my network, but not yours; it won't work for you. It's not clear from this dialog box, but the proxy and SOCKS methods are mutually exclusive. Use either the proxy method or the SOCKS method, but not both. Your system administrator can guide you here.

The No Proxy box is an item of interest. If you have Web servers *inside* your LAN, Netscape can contact them directly and needn't use the proxy. No Proxy allows you to exclude a list of servers from access through the proxy.

# OTHER NETSCAPE PREFERENCES

Many of Netscape's preferences have been described in other lessons. Those which haven't been described are outlined in this section.

## WINDOW AND LINK STYLES

You visited the Window and Link Styles Preferences dialog box in Lesson 23. Here you control several Netscape appearance aspects. These include, in addition to font size:

- Use of icons and/or text in the Toolbar

- Whether you start with a blank page or a home page

- Whether hyperlinks are underlined on-screen

- How long Netscape remembers the links you've visited (recall that links change color once you've visited them). The Now button expires all your links.

All of the changes here are cosmetic and have no real effect on how Netscape operates. Feel free to set them according to your personal preferences. (See Figure 24.2.)

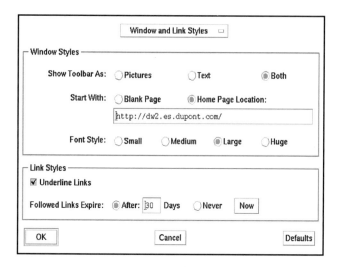

**FIGURE 24.2**    The Window and Link Styles preferences dialog box.

## CACHE AND NETWORK

The settings for Netscape's caching options were explained in Lesson 6.

In most local area network situations, the settings for Network Connections need not be changed. Check with your system administrator before changing either setting. The Cache and Network Preferences dialog box is shown in Figure 24.3

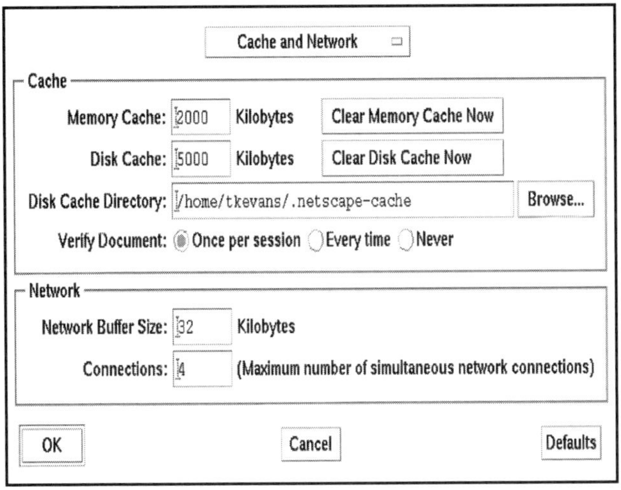

**FIGURE 24.3**    The Cache and Network preferences dialog box.

## APPLICATIONS AND DIRECTORIES

The preferences dialog box shown in Figure 24.4 is divided into two sections. Supporting Applications are special Helper applications you may need to conduct an interactive login session on a remote computer system. You'll note that the default settings open *xterm* windows, in which the telnet or rlogin commands are executed. If you prefer hpterm (on your Hewlett-Packard UNIX system) or aixterm (on your IBM AIX system), you can change these.

Netscape makes temporary copies of files it downloads; the Temporary Directory setting tells Netscape where to put them. With large audio or video files, you may run out of space in the **/tmp** directory (the default). So, you may need to change this to a directory with more space. Be sure you have the ability to create files in any directory you select. The Browse button lets you look around for other directories.

This preferences window also allows you to specify the filename of your Bookmark list (see Lesson 6). You can accept the default, or you can change it.

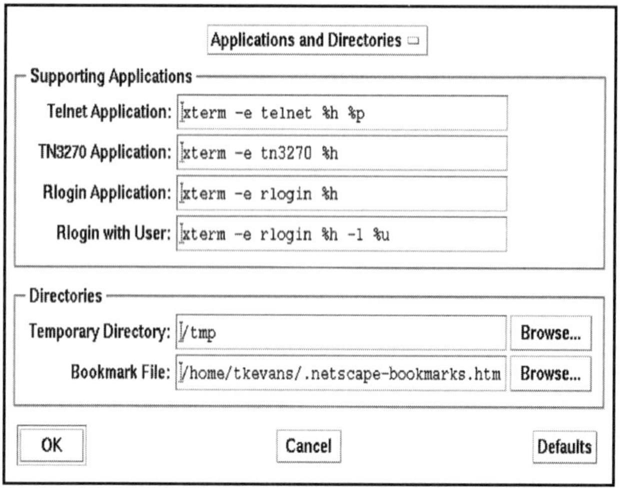

**FIGURE 24.4** The Applications and Directories preferences dialog box.

## IMAGES AND SECURITY

The Images and Security settings (see Figure 24.5) pertain to how Web page images are displayed and what security-related alerts you want to see.

You've no doubt noticed how images gradually fade in, beginning to display before they are fully downloaded. Some people think this is a great feature, while others find it irritating. Display Images allows you to turn this feature off, having Netscape wait until the entire image has been received by your computer before it is displayed.

Colors is a technical choice of how Netscape deals with downloaded images. Which of the two choices—Dithering or Use Closet Cube—you make depends on your computer hardware and on what other programs you're running at the same time as Netscape. Check both out and decide what you like best. Dithered images generally take longer to display, but may be of the best quality.

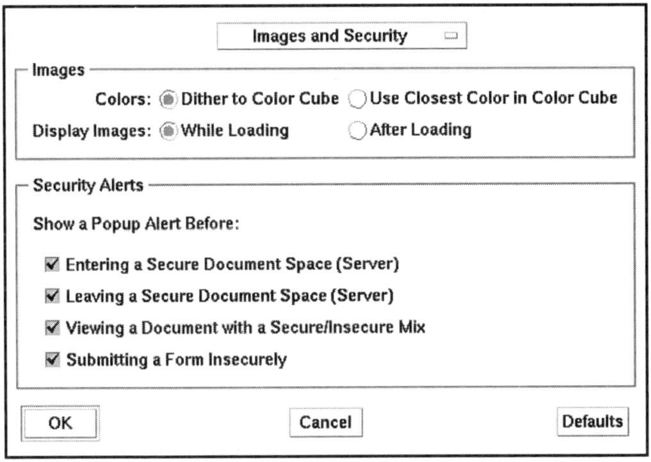

**FIGURE 24.5**    The Images and Security preferences dialog box.

You'll recall from Lesson 19 that Netscape can communicate securely with some Web servers and can also identify insecure connections. Security Alerts allow you to tell Netscape what sort of alerts, if any, to display. Click the check boxes to turn the alerts on or off.

In this lesson you learned how to configure Netscape and set preferences for the options Netscape allows you to control.

This book has introduced Netscape for UNIX systems. If you use Windows or Macintosh PCs, you may want to get Que Publishing's companion *10 Minute Guides*: *Netscape for Windows* and *Netscape for Macintosh*. As mentioned in several instances in this book, you'll find more detailed information about Netscape in the online manual.

# DOWNLOADING NETSCAPE OVER THE INTERNET

Although you can purchase Netscape in computer stores or directly from a manufacturer, you can also get a copy over the Internet using anonymous FTP or a World Wide Web browser, such as NCSA Mosaic. This appendix tells you how to do so; Appendix B tells you how to install the package once you've obtained it.

## GETTING NETSCAPE WITH ANONYMOUS FTP

If you don't already have some sort of World Wide Web browser working on your system, but are on the Internet, you can use your system's FTP utility to download a copy. The TCP/IP file-transfer protocol (FTP) is a standard part of virtually all UNIX systems. Although there are some graphical FTP "tools" available here and there for UNIX systems, they're not part of any vendor's standard UNIX installation, so we'll focus on the nongraphical user interface all provide.

 **TCP/IP**   The Transmission Control/Internet Protocols are the network language of the Internet. All the network programs you use, including Netscape, speak TCP/IP, but unless you're a network administrator, you need to know very little about the protocols.

The UNIX FTP utility is a nongraphical one. So, you'll need to run it from the shell in a terminal window, such as a Sun cmdtool,

AIX aixterm, HP-UX hpterm, standard X Windows xterm, or any
ordinary terminal session.

Figures A.1 through A.3 show the process of downloading
Netscape using anonymous FTP.

- In Figure A.1, the user logs into Netscape's anonymous
  FTP server named ftp.netscape.com, using the login name
  anonymous. For a password, type in your Internet e-mail
  address, such as yourname@yourcompany.com.

- Figure A.2 shows a directory listing from the server's
  **/netscape/unix** subdirectory, with the several different
  versions of Netscape displayed.

- Finally, Figure A.3 shows the actual download taking
  place.

In Figure A.3, note the use of the ftp pwd (print working directory) command to show we've switched to the netscape/unix
subdirectory, and the bin (binary transfer mode) command.
Finally, get netscape-v11N-export.mips-sgi-irix5.2.tar.Z downloads the SGI version of Netscape. At this point, you can download additional versions of Netscape. To end the FTP session,
just type **bye**.

```
                            xterm
/users/tkevans $ ftp ftp.netscape.com
Connected to ftp1.netscape.com.
220 ftp1.netscape.com FTP server (Version wu-2.4(3) Tue Dec 27 17:53:56 PST 1994
) ready.
Name (ftp.netscape.com:tkevans): anonymous
331 Guest login ok, send your complete e-mail address as password.
Password:
230-Welcome to the Netscape Communications Corporation FTP server.
230-
230-If you have any odd problems, try logging in with a minus sign (-)
230-as the first character of your password.  This will turn off a feature
230-that may be confusing your ftp client program.
230-
230-Please send any questions, comments, or problem reports about
230-this server to ftp@netscape.com.
230-
230 Guest login ok, access restrictions apply.
ftp> 
```

FIGURE A.1    Accessing Netscape's FTP server.

```
┌──────────────────────────────── xterm ──────────────────────────┐
│ drwxr-xr-x   5 root    sys       512 May 11 00:19 ..             │
│ -rw-rw-r--   1 root    sys      1445 Jun 20 16:23 .message       │
│ -rw-r--r--   1 root    sys      6926 Apr 24 23:57 LICENSE        │
│ -rw-r--r--   1 root    sys      5871 Apr 24 23:58 README         │
│ -rw-r--r--   1 root    sys   2698027 Apr 24 23:57 netscape-v11N-export.alph│
│ a-dec-osf2.0.tar.Z                                              │
│ -rw-r--r--   1 root    sys   2184141 Apr 24 23:57 netscape-v11N-export.hppa│
│ 1.1-hp-hpux.tar.Z                                              │
│ -rw-r--r--   1 root    sys   1647267 Apr 24 23:57 netscape-v11N-export.i386│
│ -unknown-bsd.tar.Z                                             │
│ -rw-r--r--   1 root    sys   1610421 Apr 24 23:57 netscape-v11N-export.i486│
│ -unknown-linux.tar.Z                                          │
│ -rw-r--r--   1 root    sys   1049463 Apr 24 23:57 netscape-v11N-export.mips│
│ -sgi-irix5.2.tar.Z                                            │
│ -rw-r--r--   1 root    sys   1028871 Apr 24 23:57 netscape-v11N-export.rs60│
│ 00-ibm-aix3.2.tar.Z                                           │
│ -rw-r--r--   1 root    sys   1749959 Apr 24 23:57 netscape-v11N-export.spar│
│ c-sun-solaris2.3.tar.Z                                        │
│ -rw-r--r--   1 root    sys   3706310 Apr 24 23:57 netscape-v11N-export.spar│
│ c-sun-sunos4.1.3_U1.tar.Z                                     │
│ 226 Transfer complete.                                        │
│ remote: netscape/unix                                        │
│ 1135 bytes received in 0.95 seconds (1.2 Kbytes/s)           │
│ ftp> ▊                                                        │
└──────────────────────────────────────────────────────────────┘
```

FIGURE A.2    Displaying a directory listing on Netscape's FTP server.

```
┌──────────────────────────────── xterm ──────────────────────────┐
│ ftp>                                                           │
│ ftp>                                                           │
│ ftp>                                                           │
│ ftp>                                                           │
│ ftp>                                                           │
│ ftp>                                                           │
│ ftp>                                                           │
│ ftp>                                                           │
│ ftp>                                                           │
│ ftp>                                                           │
└──────────────────────────────────────────────────────────────┘
```

FIGURE A.3    Downloading a copy of Netscape for UNIX.

## DOWNLOADING NETSCAPE WITH ANOTHER WEB BROWSER

If you already have a Web browser installed on your system, you can use it to retrieve Netscape. For example, in NCSA Mosaic, pull down the File menu and select Open URL. When the dialog box opens up, type in the URL **ftp://ftp.netscape.com/netscape/ unix**. This will take you directly to the subdirectory on Netscape's anonymous FTP server containing the various UNIX versions. Figure A.4 shows this directory.

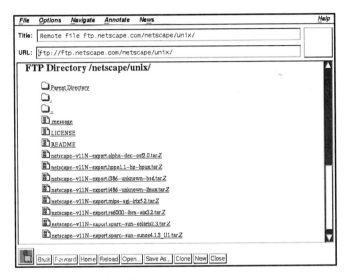

**Figure A.4**    Using NCSA Mosaic to access Netscape's FTP server.

To download a copy, pull down the Options menu and select Save to Local Disk; then click the version you want. Once the download is complete, a dialog box will open up, prompting you to enter the filename to save the download under. Continue to click any other versions you want to download. Exit from Mosaic when you're finished.

# What to Do with the Downloaded File

As you've noticed, the file you've downloaded using either the manual FTP process or a Web browser has a name ending in .Z. This means the file has been processed using a UNIX file-compression utility to make it smaller, so it doesn't take so long to download. You need to restore the file to its original condition before proceeding. Do this with the UNIX uncompress command:

> **# uncompress netscape-v11N-export.mips-sgi-irix5.2.tar.Z**

This will decompress the file and rename it netscape-v11N-export.mips-sgi-irix5.2.tar. The trailing .Z is gone. Appendix B gives details on installing Netscape.

# Notes About Netscape Versions and Licensing

The examples in this appendix (and in the rest of book as well) use Version 1.1 of Netscape. By the time you read this book, later versions may be available. In fact, Version 1.2 is currently in Beta Test for Microsoft Windows and for the Macintosh.

In addition, you'll note all the versions available for download via anonymous FTP on the Internet have the word *export* in their names. These versions of Netscape, which can be exported anywhere in the world, *are not fully capable of secure World Wide Web transactions* (see Lesson 19). This is because the U.S. Government prohibits export of the data encryption technology contained in the secure version of Netscape. If you need the fully secure version of Netscape and are in the United States, the only way you can obtain it is to purchase it.

Finally, be sure to read and understand Netscape's licensing terms. Netscape is free for many users, but others are required to pay for it.

# INSTALLING
# NETSCAPE ON A
# UNIX SYSTEM

# B

Although you can install Netscape in your own
user directory on a UNIX system, you'll probably want to get your
system administrator to install it. This will make it accessible to
everyone else using the system.

**System Administrator?** Unlike PC operating systems,
UNIX systems are multi-user, multi-tasking computers.
Since they're more complex than PCs, UNIX systems
usually need trained system administrators to maintain
them.

As you've already learned, you can download Netscape over the
Internet using FTP. You can also, of course, purchase Netscape
directly. If you purchase Netscape for UNIX, it comes on a
CD-ROM. We'll first describe how to extract the Netscape files
from the CD-ROM, and then describe how to install the package.

## INSTALLING NETSCAPE
## FROM CD-ROM

The Netscape CD-ROM contains separate versions for several different UNIX systems, all of which run X Windows:

- Sun Microsystems (SunOS 4.1.x and Solaris 2.x)

- IBM RISC System 6000 (AIX 3.2.5)

- BSDI and Linux (two versions of UNIX for IBM-
  compatible PCs)

- Digital's OSF/1 (now called Digital UNIX)

- Silicon Graphics (IRIX 5.x)

- Hewlett-Packard (HP-UX 9.x)

Here's a UNIX-style directory listing of the CD-ROM's top-level directory:

```
-r--r--r--   1  root   6074   Apr 21  01:27  _readme.txt
dr-xr-xr-x   2  root   2048   Apr 21  01:12  aix.32
drwxr-xr-x   2  root   2048   Apr 24  12:40  bsdi
dr-xr-xr-x   3  root   2048   Apr 21  01:16  common
dr-xr-xr-x   2  root   2048   Apr 21  01:15  dec_osf1.20
dr-xr-xr-x   2  root   2048   Apr 21  01:15  hpux.903
dr-xr-xr-x   2  root   2048   Apr 21  01:15  irix.52
-r--r--r--   1  root   9351   Apr 19  11:40  license.txt
drwxr-xr-x   2  root   2048   Apr 24  12:15  linux
dr-xr-xr-x   2  root   2048   Apr 21  01:15  solaris.23
dr-xr-xr-x   2  root   2048   Apr 21  01:15  sunos.413
```

As you can see, there's a readme.txt document on the CD, which you'll want to read. This is a plain text file that you can print or display on-screen with the **more** or **pg** commands.

Each of the supported systems has a different procedure for loading (called *mounting* in UNIX-speak) the CD-ROM. You may need your system administrator's help and, of course, you need a system with a CD-ROM drive available. (You don't need a CD player on every system, because you can install Netscape from one machine to another over your local area network.)

Once the CD-ROM is mounted, the procedure for installing Netscape is pretty much the same on all systems. Let's get the CD-ROM mounted first, and then turn to the installation.

## MOUNTING THE **CD-ROM** ON SUN SYSTEMS

On a Sun system running SunOS 4.1.x (also called Solaris 1.x), you'll need access to the *root*, or super-user, account to mount the CD-ROM. Once you or your system administrator is logged into the root account, insert the CD-ROM into its caddy and place it in the CD player; then type the following commands (the **#** symbol represents the super-user prompt; you don't enter it):

> **# mkdir /cdrom**
>
> **# /etc/mount -rt hsfs /dev/sr0 /cdrom**

The system may tell you the /cdrom directory already exists; you can ignore this message.

Double-check that the mount succeeded by asking for a directory listing with the command **ls /cdrom**.

On a Sun system running Solaris 2.x (also called SunOS 5.x), you may or may not need super-user authority to mount the CD-ROM, depending on how the system was configured when it was installed. Ask your system administrator if the Solaris Volume Management feature is enabled. If so, you can simply slip the CD-ROM into the player and the system will automatically mount it for you. After a couple of minutes, you'll be able to change to the **/cdrom/cdrom0** directory and see the Netscape CD.

If Volume Management is not running on your Solaris 2.x system, mounting the CD-ROM requires super-user access. Use the following commands:

> **# mkdir /cdrom**
>
> **# mount -o ro -F hsfs /dev/dsk/c0t6d0s2 /cdrom**

Double-check that the mount succeeded by asking for a directory listing with the command **ls /cdrom**.

## MOUNTING THE CD-ROM ON AN IBM AIX SYSTEM

IBM's UNIX, called AIX, also requires super-user authority to mount CD-ROMs, but there's a pretty friendly interface to do so, using the System Management Interface Tool, or *smit*. Start up smit, select Physical and Logical Storage, Filesystems, and then finally Mount a Filesystem. Fill in the blanks, and then click DO to mount the CD-ROM.

## MOUNTING THE CD-ROM ON A SILICON GRAPHICS SYSTEM

SIG's UNIX, called IRIX, automatically senses and mounts the CD-ROM when it is placed into the CD player. Just pop the CD-ROM in and it will be mounted on the directory /CDROM.

## MOUNTING THE CD-ROM ON AN HP-UX SYSTEM

HP-UX 9.x requires manual mounting of CD-ROM filesystems. Here's the super-user command to do so:

```
# mkdir /cdrom
# mount -rt cdfs /dev/dsk/c201d2s0 /cdrom
```

## MOUNTING THE CD-ROM ON A BSDI SYSTEM

This is the super-user command for mounting of CDs on a BSDI system:

```
# mount_cd9660 /dev/sd6a /cdrom
```

## MOUNTING THE CD-ROM ON A LINUX SYSTEM

Linux also requires manual mounting of CDs, by the super-user. Use these commands:

```
# mkdir /cdrom
# mount -rt iso9660 /dev/scd0 /cdrom
```

## MOUNTING THE CD-ROM ON A DEC OSF/1 SYSTEM

Digital UNIX requires manual mounting of CD-ROM filesystems. Here's the super-user command to do so:

```
# mkdir /cdrom

# mount -rt cdfs /dev/rz6c /cdrom
```

# INSTALLING NETSCAPE

Whether you've downloaded Netscape over the Internet or purchased it on CD-ROM, you're now ready to install the package. With some small differences, which are noted below, It's assumed you're operating as root, the super-user. Here are the steps:

1. Note the directory in which the Netscape *tar* archive file is located (/cdrom/aix.32/netscape.tar, for example, on an IBM RS/6000, or the directory into which you downloaded Netscape via ftp).

2. Change to a directory with at least 5M of free space and run the following command, substituting the correct directory for /cdrom/aix.32:

```
# tar xfv /cdrom/aix.32/netscape.tar
```

   You now have several files in your working directory, including files called netscape, LICENSE, README, Netscape.ad, XKeysymDB, and hot-convert.sh.

3. Move the Netscape executable program into a directory accessible to all users on your system. A common place is the /usr/local/bin directory. Here's the command:

```
# mv netscape /usr/local/bin
```

4. Move the Netscape application defaults file into a central location on the system:

```
# mv Netscape.ad /usr/lib/X11/app-defaults/
Netscape
```

**Directory /usr/lib/X11 Doesn't Exist!**   If you can't find **/usr/lib/X11**, you're probably on a Sun system, on which the app-defaults directory is **/usr/openwin/lib/X11/ app-defaults**. Place the file in this directory instead.

5. Move the key symbols file into a central location on the system:

    # mv XKeysymDB /usr/lib/X11

**Key Symbols?**   This is a particularly important file for Sun users, since Netscape is a **Motif** application. Because most Sun users use Sun's **OpenWindows** graphical user interface, the supplied XKeysymDB file, which replaces the standard Sun version, contains the needed Motif keyboard bindings. If you don't install this file, Netscape will generate a large number of error messages on startup and some of the keystrokes may not work properly (or may not work at all).

6. If people on your system have been using NCSA Mosaic for Web browsing, they'll want to make their Mosaic Hotlists work as Netscape Bookmarks. To enable them to do so, install the supplied conversion file:

    # mv hot-convert.sh /usr/local/bin

You're done installing Netscape. Exit from your current X Windows session and start a new one to effectuate all the changes.

# Index